THE SOCIAL MEDIA DETOX TRACKER

A Journal to **Stop Mindless Scrolling, Set Healthy Goals**, and **Take Back Your Time!**

COURTNEY E. ACKERMAN

ADAMS MEDIA

NEW YORK   LONDON   TORONTO   SYDNEY   NEW DELHI

Adams Media
An Imprint of Simon & Schuster, Inc.
100 Technology Center Drive
Stoughton, Massachusetts 02072

First Adams Media trade paperback edition August 2022

ADAMS MEDIA and colophon are trademarks of Simon & Schuster.

For information about special discounts for bulk purchases, please contact Simon & Schuster Special Sales at 1-866-506-1949 or business@ simonandschuster.com.

The Simon & Schuster Speakers Bureau can bring authors to your live event. For more information or to book an event contact the Simon & Schuster Speakers Bureau at 1-866-248-3049 or visit our website at www.simonspeakers.com.

Interior design by Colleen Cunningham and Julia Jacintho

Manufactured in the United States of America

1 2022

ISBN 978-1-5072-1963-8

CONTENTS

INTRODUCTION

It's easy to lose track of time on social media—after all, it's designed to keep you engaged at all times with must-see content. Whether you're checking out your friends' gorgeous vacation pics, scrolling through motivational stories and quotes, watching the funny video clip everyone's talking about, or posting your own share-worthy quips and photos, you can easily lose hours on one of the many available apps. But is that a healthy way to spend your precious spare time?

You probably already know that using social media too often can have negative side effects, like poor sleep, increased anxiety, poor academic or work performance, and even symptoms of depression. But how much is too much social media? How often are you using it? Should you give up social media completely, or just cut down the amount of time you spend on it? And how do you even start cutting back?

If you're asking these questions, you're not alone. Social media usage is a problem for many of us, especially as apps get more and more efficient at capturing our attention. With *The Social Media Detox Tracker*, you will assess your current habits, spend time away from social media, and take control of your scrolling habit, then mindfully re-engage in a way that works for you and your mental health.

This interactive guide lets you set goals and lead the way, but provides information, support, and encouragement along your journey. In Part 1, you'll learn about how social media can interfere with your well-being and why tracking your usage can be eye-opening. As you track your experiences, you'll get a full picture of which parts of social media are adding to your life and which parts you can do without. In Part 2 of this book, you'll slowly reduce your usage of social media for three days, then avoid it completely for seven days, all while using journal pages to record your experiences as you disengage from your apps and live in the present. Then in Part 3, you'll decide exactly how much and in what ways you want to reintegrate social media into your life. You'll record your goal for social media minutes, track your moods, and reflect on your social media experiences as they relate to your mental health.

Are you ready to get started building a healthier social media habit? It's time to stop mindlessly scrolling and get back to your life!

PART ONE

SOCIAL MEDIA AND YOU

WHAT IS YOUR CURRENT RELATIONSHIP
WITH SOCIAL MEDIA?

Many of us have slipped into mindless relationships with social media, using it automatically without thinking about how much or how often we're using it, or how it's affecting us. There are many different ways to use social media apps, and everyone's relationship will look a little bit different. The first step to making sure social media fits into your life in a healthy way is to take some time to understand your relationship with it.

For example, many of us use social media to feel connected to others and to stay up-to-date with our friends, families, and groups or topics we're interested in. It's a great tool for seeing what our favorite people, companies, and organizations are up to and engaging with other like-minded individuals. However, we can also use it to distract ourselves from things that are painful or unpleasant in our life. Think about when you pick up your phone to scroll through Instagram or TikTok: How are you usually feeling when you do this? Is it when you feel upset or lonely? Why do you think you turn to social media to address those feelings?

HOW SOCIAL MEDIA CAN IMPACT
YOUR MENTAL HEALTH

Social media can connect us more efficiently than ever. In some cases, those connections are heartwarming and positive. But many other connections are not high-quality, kind, or meaningful, and they can leave you feeling stressed, angry, or sad. For example, many people, particularly teens and young adults, follow influencers and celebrities who showcase glamorous, glittery lives that are impossibly out of reach. The feelings of jealousy and FOMO (fear of missing out) triggered by following these accounts are totally normal, but they can lead to a sense of inadequacy and dissatisfaction with your own life.

And not only can social media make you feel like you're missing out or falling behind, but it can give you really skewed perceptions of what's normal and healthy. The use of filters and photo editing is ubiquitous but it can also be subtle, slowly shifting your idea of what a healthy and attainable waistline looks like or how smooth and poreless skin should be. If you're constantly consuming content that is filtered, photoshopped, and expertly angled, it's easy to forget what "normal" is—and that can lead to poor self-image, low self-esteem, and general emotional discomfort.

Furthermore, studies have shown that misusing or overusing social media can lead to disruptions and delays in your sleep, memory problems, and even impaired performance at school or work. If you're constantly checking in on your follows and counting your likes, you don't leave much room for anything else, whether that's focusing on school, completing a big project at work, or even getting the relaxing downtime you need.

It's totally normal to be drawn to social media when you feel bored, upset, or anxious. But unfortunately, social media doesn't always help you manage these feelings. It might provide a temporary relief from whatever uncomfortable thing you're feeling, but it generally isn't a long-term fix. Part of what you'll do in this book is identify other activities (besides social media) that might help you manage your mental health more effectively. You'll learn more about this later in this part and in Part 2.

HOW TO KNOW IF SOCIAL MEDIA
IS A PROBLEM FOR YOU

What counts as "too much" social media? The answer is different for everyone, depending on your habits and needs. There is no hard-and-fast rule about how much is too much. If your job requires using social media or you're a freelancer who uses Instagram or Facebook to promote yourself, your "normal and healthy" usage might be different from those of people who are just scrolling for fun.

But if you're questioning your relationship with social media, it's a good idea to keep an eye on a few of the signs associated with overdoing it. If you notice any of the following things, social media might be a problem for you:

- You're so absorbed in your phone that you miss what your friends and family are saying around you.

- You find yourself thinking, "That would make a great share/post!" all the time.

- You obsess over the likes or comments you get, tracking them carefully.

- You find yourself mindlessly scrolling multiple times a day.

- You notice that you've become more critical of appearances, either your own or others'.

- Your conversations with friends and family revolve around things you see on social media.

- You feel sad, anxious, or uncomfortable when using social media.

- You feel sad, anxious, or uncomfortable when you are in a situation where you *can't* use social media (like during an exam, when you don't have service, or when your phone dies).

- You're withdrawing from opportunities for face-to-face social interaction.

- You notice you're using social media to avoid real-life responsibilities, like work, homework, or chores.

- You feel like you're getting worse at dealing with people in real life.

- You find yourself scrolling far past the point when you should have turned off the light and gone to sleep.

- Your fingers automatically click on your social media apps whenever you pick up your phone.

- You can't stop picking up your phone!

If more than a few of these signs resonate with you, that's a good indication that your relationship with social media may be unhealthy.

HOW TRACKING YOUR SOCIAL MEDIA USAGE CAN BE HELPFUL

If you think you have an issue with social media, tracking your usage is a great place to start. It's important to get a good understanding of a problem before you set goals and start to tackle it, and that's what tracking can do for you!

Fortunately, there are tons of options for tracking your social media usage, including apps, timers, and journaling. Using these tools, you can get an idea of what your "normal" is, make an informed decision about your goal usage, and begin finding a happy balance that works for you.

Using your phone to track your social media usage is probably going to be the easiest method. Before you get started on your detox journey, make sure you know where to find your tracking data—your phone likely has built-in tracking features already. If you have a newer Android, check for the Digital Wellbeing app. If you have an iPhone, the tracking feature is called Screen Time. If your phone doesn't have one of these features built in, you can try one of the many free apps for tracking your time, like Moment, App Usage, or QualityTime.

Whatever option you choose, make sure to spend some time getting familiar with it so you're ready to hit the ground running on Day 1.

WHAT TO DO INSTEAD OF SOCIAL MEDIA

If you've ever tried to quit or cut down on a habit before, you know that it's often tough to just *stop* doing something without actively replacing it with something else. As you start thinking about this detox, ask yourself: "If I'm not using social media, what can I do to fill my time and distract myself from what I may be missing?"

The list of options is nearly endless, and it will be unique to you. You'll want to fill your time with things that appeal to you, will help you grow, and can keep your mind off scrolling.

Here's just a sample of the things you might choose to do instead of using social media:

- Journaling
- Meditating
- Calling or video chatting with a friend
- Doing a crossword puzzle, Sudoku, or other brainteasing activity
- Dancing
- Reading a book
- Taking a walk
- Practicing active mindfulness
- Listening to music
- Watching a TV show or movie
- Gardening
- Cooking
- Cleaning
- Researching the latest topic you're interested in
- Organizing or reorganizing your clothes, a room, etc.
- Stretching
- Practicing a musical instrument
- Painting, drawing, or coloring
- Knitting or crocheting
- Playing a board game or card game
- Learning a new skill

This list of activities is diverse, and not even close to complete, but you might notice something about it: They are all *active and intentional* options—and that's the key. Mindlessly scrolling social media is easy because it just *happens*, with almost no effort. To change that habit, the best method is to do the opposite: Actively choose to engage in alternative activities. You'll think more about the best activities for you while filling out the journal pages in Part 2.

PART TWO

SOCIAL MEDIA DETOX

UNDERSTANDING THE TEN-DAY SOCIAL MEDIA DETOX

Social media can be tough to detox from since it's everywhere! But this easy-to-follow ten-day plan will help you put down the phone and re-engage with the world around you. And don't worry: Your end goal doesn't need to be "stop using social media and never use it again." There are healthy ways to fit social media into your life.

WHY TEN DAYS?

This detox is scheduled for ten days to make it manageable while also effective. Depending on who you ask, it takes somewhere between ten and twenty-one days to build a new habit. While this detox isn't necessarily meant to help you *build* new habits (although that's often a side effect of reducing social media usage), it is designed to help you *break* an unhelpful habit, which can happen quicker.

You can certainly refrain from using social media for longer than ten days if you choose to! But in today's world, that may not be practical for many people who use social media to keep up with friends and family, promote themselves and their work, or do their job. Plus, while two weeks (or longer) would be more effective in breaking the social media habit entirely, that's not the main goal of this detox. The aim is to build a *healthier relationship* with social media, in a life that requires at least some social media usage. For this purpose, ten days is a perfect balance.

You'll do this detox in three main steps:

1. Use **Day 1** to track your social media usage and gain an understanding of your relationship with social media.

2. You'll wind down your social media usage on **Days 2–3**, then take a weeklong break from it **(Days 4–10)**, all while learning more about yourself.

3. After the ten days are done, you'll take what you've learned and apply it to your life as you mindfully re-engage with social media.

Each step has a specific purpose. The first step allows you to see where you stand now. Before you can change your relationship with social media, you first need to know what your current relationship is like. In this step, you'll track and assess your phone usage, thinking about how it affects you, when you use it, why you use it, and what sort of habits might work better for you.

In the second step, you'll take a couple of days to wind down your usage. Once you've tapered down your usage, you'll stop using social media entirely for seven days. But that's not your only task during this time! You'll also be thinking about your experience, journaling, and exploring other activities that you can do instead of using social media.

Finally, after you've completed your weeklong detox, you'll work on creating a plan for more mindful and intentional social media usage going forward.

MENTALLY PREPARING FOR THE DETOX

As you gear up to start your social media detox, it's a good idea to get mentally prepared. To do that, try a little introspection: Think about yourself, your thoughts and feelings on social media, and why you're using social media. This section will walk you through that process.

WHY ARE YOU DOING WHAT YOU'RE DOING?

In the days leading up to the beginning of your social media detox, start to pay more attention to your thoughts, your feelings, and your urges, particularly those involving using social media. When and where are you most likely to use it? Do you use it mindlessly, scrolling without a purpose, or do you use it mindfully, to connect and to learn? Try to be honest with yourself. Are you starting to notice any patterns around your habit?

It is also helpful to focus on why you want to change your relationship with social media. Some of the questions in this part will prompt reflection on this topic, but you may want to do some extra thinking on it as you go. If you know *why* you want to achieve a goal, it'll be much easier to work toward!

THINK ABOUT YOUR INTENTIONS

Once you start to pay more attention to your thoughts, feelings, and behaviors, you'll build a better understanding of yourself and your challenges, which will make you more effective in creating a healthier relationship with social media and with yourself. With this knowledge in hand, you'll be more aware and ready to focus on meeting your goals.

You'll find space on the journal pages to record your intentions about social media usage. Thinking about what you like and dislike and what works for you and what doesn't will help you create intentions that are best suited for your personality and needs. For example, you might want to work on being more mindful of the world around you. In that case, your intention may be: "Every time I want to use social media, I will look up instead. I will find five things that are interesting, unique, or pleasant to look at around me." If you want to work on being more self-aware, you might set an intention like: "I will pause and check in with myself to see what I'm feeling at least three times tomorrow." If you're still winding down or back to using social media mindfully, you might set an intention around the type of content you will engage with, such as: "I will only scroll through positive and uplifting accounts on social media tomorrow."

THE STEP-DOWN APPROACH

Although the full detox takes ten days, you'll notice that you don't need to completely avoid social media at the beginning of the ten-day period. You'll start by spending one day tracking your usage, then cut down on your social media usage for two days, then transition to zero social media for the last seven days. With this method, you have some time to get used to the reduction in social media usage and solidify your reasons for wanting to change your relationship with social media.

During the step-down days, you should base your social media usage goal on your current regular usage, via the following formula:

- **Day 1:** Just track

- **Day 2:** Cut usage by 50 percent

- **Day 3:** Cut usage by 75 percent

Then on Day 4, you'll begin a full detox of any social media apps. This step-by-step method will help you prepare for cutting social media usage out entirely, while giving you time to be mindful and learn more about yourself and your usage.

GUIDELINES FOR DETOXING

As you begin your detox, keep the following guidelines in mind:

- Rate your morning mood as soon as you get up each morning and before you get started with your day.

- Complete the rest of the journal page and rate your evening mood at the end of the day, just before getting ready for bed.

- Answer the questions about social media usage honestly. If you trip up and use social media during the last seven days, just notice when and why it happened and record that on your journal page. Avoid judging or shaming yourself. We all make mistakes! Offer yourself kindness and compassion, and approach your slipup with curiosity instead of judgment. Consider when and why you slipped up, what drove you to it, and how you can avoid slipping up again in the future. Remind yourself that this is a learning experience, not a pass/fail class!

- Stay in touch with your emotions during the detox. It's totally understandable if you feel a little down, bored, lonely, or any other negative feelings while you're detoxing, but it's important to be aware of your feelings and reflect on them. It can also be helpful to share them with others. (On Day 2, you'll choose a detox buddy whom you can go to for support and accountability. This would be a great person to share your thoughts and feelings with during this time.)

- The more reflection involved, the better—so don't shy away from getting wordy! Write as much as you need to, and expand on your thoughts, feelings, and ideas as much as you can. If you need to continue on another page in your own journal, go for it.

- Each day builds on what you've learned or experienced in previous days, so make sure to complete them in order.

- If you find yourself using social media too often again, you can always start the ten-day detox over. Just use fresh pages of a journal or notebook to respond to the prompts on the ten-day detox pages.

Enough preparation—you're ready to begin the detox! Grab a pen or pencil and get started with Day 1.

DAY 1 Date: / /

Tracking Your Time

SOCIAL MEDIA USAGE

Goal Time: Actual Time:

Other:
_____

In the past, how have you felt while using social media and afterward?

O Connected
O Irritated
O Happy
O Anxious
O Refreshed
O Uneasy
O Sad
O Jealous
O Lonely
O Energized
O Insecure
O _____

Why do you want to do a ten-day detox from social media?
Clarify your reasons for detoxing.

....
....
....

What do you think will be the hardest part of detoxing?
List your challenges.

....
....
....

What do you think will help you stick to detoxing and make the most of it?
List your resources.

....
....
....
....
....
....

DAY 2   Date: /   /

Begin Tapering Down

○ 😣 ○ 😟 ○ 😐 ○ 🙂 ○ 😊

Goal Time: Actual Time:

How are you feeling about
your detox plan today?

Other:
_____

When did you find yourself most
drawn to social media?

What is your intention for cutting down
on social media usage tomorrow?

Why do you think you felt drawn to it
at those times?

Is there anyone in your life who would
be a good detox buddy on this journey?

○ 😣 ○ 😟 ○ 😐 ○ 🙂 ○ 😊

Finish Tapering Down

Goal Time: Actual Time:

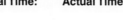

Other:

_____

How have you felt in the past few days while using social media and afterward?

O Connected
O Irritated
O Happy
O Anxious
O Refreshed
O Uneasy
O Sad
O Jealous
O Lonely
O Energized
O Insecure
O _____

Is there anything you miss while using social media less often?

....
....
....

Are there any needs you feel aren't being met?

....
....
....

What can you do instead of using social media to get those needs met?

....
....
....

Did you check in with your detox buddy today?

O Yes   O No

If yes, how did that go?

....
....
....

If no, why not?

....
....
....

DAY 4   Date: /   /

Using Zero Social Media

Did you use social media today?

○ Yes   ○ No

If you did...

When?

Why?

Was it difficult to avoid using social media today?

○ Yes   ○ No

If so...

When?

Why?

How would you rate your experience with this detox so far?

○ Very negative

○ Somewhat negative

○ Neutral

○ Somewhat positive

○ Very positive

Think about why you rated your experience as you did. What makes it negative or positive so far?

Has avoiding social media today impacted your mood?

○ Yes   ○ No

If yes, how?

If no, why?

○ 😠 ○ ☹️ ○ 😐 ○ 🙂 ○ 😊

DAY 5 Date: /   /

Brainstorming Alternative Activities

SOCIAL MEDIA USAGE

Did you use social media today?

O Yes   O No

If you did...

When? ....

....

....

Why? ....

....

....

What have you been doing instead of using social media?

O Journaling
O Spending time with friends
O Meditating
O Spending time outside
O Learning something new
O Cooking
O Cleaning
O Reading
O Playing video games
O Watching TV/movies
O _____
O _____

What has been your favorite use of time over the last two days?

....

....

Why? ....

....

....

Do you still find yourself missing social media?

O Yes   O No

If yes, when?

....

....

Have you felt more productive, more relaxed, or calmer?

O Yes   O No

If yes, do you think some of that is due to replacing social media with other activities?

O Yes   O No

How much?

....

....

EVENING MOOD TRACKER

O 😣 O 😦 O 😐 O 🙂 O 😊

DAY 6   Date: /   /

Building Awareness

○ 😠 ○ 🙁 ○ 😐 ○ 🙂 ○ 😊

Have you noticed other people mindlessly scrolling through social media in the last few days?

○ Yes   ○ No

If yes, what thoughts or feelings did it bring up for you?

....

....

....

SOCIAL MEDIA USAGE

Did you use social media today?

○ Yes   ○ No

If you did...

When? ....

....

....

Why? ....

....

....

What have you noticed about the *world around you* today that you might not have noticed if you were busy using social media?

....

....

....

....

In general, how do you feel when you notice you are tempted to use social media?

....

....

....

....

....

Have you learned anything new?

....

....

....

....

....

What have you noticed about *yourself* over the last day of not using social media?

....

....

....

....

....

○ 😠 ○ 🙁 ○ 😐 ○ 🙂 ○ 😊

TODAY'S FOCUS:

Your Feelings Toward Social Media

MORNING MOOD TRACKER

SOCIAL MEDIA USAGE

Did you use social media today?

○ Yes   ○ No

If you did...

When? ....

....

....

Why? ....

....

....

How do you feel about social media today?

....

....

....

Has your attitude toward social media changed?

○ Yes   ○ No

What do you think you get from using social media?

....

....

....

In general, how have you felt over the last week?

○ Connected
○ Irritated
○ Happy
○ Anxious
○ Refreshed
○ Uneasy
○ Sad
○ Jealous
○ Lonely
○ Energized
○ Insecure
○ _____

What wants or needs does it meet?

....

....

Do you think social media is a good way to get those wants or needs met?

○ Yes   ○ No

Why or why not?

....

....

EVENING MOOD TRACKER

You've been detoxing from social media for a full week! Way to go!

DAY 8   Date: /   /

Trying New Things

○ 😣 ○ 🙁 ○ 😐 ○ 🙂 ○ 😊

Did you use social media today?

○ Yes   ○ No

If you did...

When?

Why?

Have you noticed any changes in how you feel about yourself since you started this detox?

○ Yes   ○ No

If yes, what changes have you noticed?

What *new activities* have you picked up (or what old activities have you picked up again) in the last eight days?

How do you feel while doing these activities?

What is your intention for tomorrow?

Is there anything specific you want to work on?

○ 😣 ○ 🙁 ○ 😐 ○ 🙂 ○ 😊

DAY 9 Date: / /

Cultivating Gratitude

SOCIAL MEDIA USAGE

Did you use social media today?

○ Yes   ○ No

If you did...

When? ....

....

....

Why? ....

....

....

....

What are you most grateful for today? Make a list.

....

....

....

....

....

....

....

....

....

....

....

....

MORNING MOOD TRACKER

○ 😣 ○ 🙁 ○ 😐 ○ 🙂 ○ 😊

What techniques or strategies have worked best for you so far?

....

....

....

Did you check in with your detox buddy today?

○ Yes   ○ No

If yes, how did that go?

....

....

....

If no, why not?

....

....

Do you find it easier to be grateful when you are not using social media?

○ Yes   ○ No

Why or why not?

....

....

....

EVENING MOOD TRACKER

○ 😣 ○ 🙁 ○ 😐 ○ 🙂 ○ 😊

DAY 10 Date: /   /

TODAY'S FOCUS:

Practicing Mindfulness

SOCIAL MEDIA USAGE

Did you use social media today?

O Yes   O No

If you did...

When?

Why?

How do you feel about yourself now that you've completed the ten-day detox?

Do you feel your relationship with social media has changed?

O Yes   O No

If yes, how?

MORNING MOOD TRACKER

O 😣 O 😦 O 😐 O 🙂 O 😊

Do you feel you've become more mindful in your normal day-to-day life?

O Yes   O No

If yes, how?

How do you want to mindfully engage with social media going forward?

Write out a plan.

EVENING MOOD TRACKER

O 😣 O 😦 O 😐 O 🙂 O 😊

You've completed your ten-day detox! Congratulations!

RE-ENGAGING WITH SOCIAL MEDIA

CONGRATULATIONS! LOOKING AHEAD

You did it! You made it through your ten-day detox, and along the way you learned a whole lot about yourself and how you relate to social media. Perhaps you found new hobbies (or rediscovered old ones), or maybe you reconnected to the world around you in a new, more mindful way. Now it's time to apply that knowledge as you establish a better, healthier relationship with social media going forward.

Using your experience over the last ten days, think about how you want to use social media now. Based on the reflections you've been doing in your journaling, what do you think is a healthy amount of social media usage? Or a healthy type of usage? Do you want to make some changes to the accounts you follow, frequent, or friend? Use your newfound understanding of yourself to build a healthy social media plan that's customized for you. Consider what apps you want to use, how often you want to use them, and what kinds of content you want to engage with and/or post on your social media accounts. Write your plan in the space here.

Remember, the goal doesn't have to be to avoid social media for-ever—it's perfectly fine to use it in a way that works best for you. The key? Mindfulness.

SOCIAL MEDIA USAGE	Plan Notes:
Goal Time:	

Other:
_____

Plan Notes:

What kinds of content do I want to engage with?

Do I need to unfollow or begin following any accounts based on my new knowledge?

What kinds of content do I want to post on my own social media accounts?

Your main goal now is probably *not* to avoid using social media. It may not even be to use social media *less* than you were pre-detox, per se. Your main goal should be to use social media more *mindfully*. Being mindful of social media usage means knowing your current state of mind, understanding your reasons for using social media, and making informed decisions about how and when to use it.

Instead of mindlessly scrolling through pics on Instagram or getting sucked into a TikTok binge, you can open your social media apps for a specific purpose, fulfill that purpose, then close the app and move on with your day.

How do you do this? Every time you are tempted to open up a social media app on your phone, pause and take a moment to ask yourself questions like:

1. How am I feeling right now? What specific emotions am I experiencing?

2. Why do I want to use social media? What is my goal? Do I even have a particular goal or am I just bored/lonely/uncomfortable/looking to pass time?

3. Do I need to accomplish this goal right now?

4. Do I need to use social media to accomplish this goal? Is there another option?

5. How long do I expect to need to use social media during this instance? When will I exit the app?

6. What will I do after I use social media? What's my plan for avoiding mindless scrolling?

Asking yourself these questions may feel a bit burdensome at first, but it will quickly become second nature. You can also write down your feelings using the journal pages in this part.

CHECKING IN WITH YOURSELF

As you feel out your new relationship with social media, there may be some trial and error. That's okay! You can balance and readjust as needed. The journal pages in this part will help you know what adjustments you need. You can use the pages to:

- Assess your morning mood.
- Set an intention for your social media use based on your needs and goals.
- Track your social media goal time versus the actual time spent on social media.
- Note what you did instead of using social media.
- Help you visualize the effects of social media on your mood—are you staying cool and calm, or becoming hot-tempered and upset? (Shade in the thermometer icon accordingly.)
- Gauge how your social media use is making you feel, so you can stay aware of its effect on you and set a goal for the next day.

You can also reflect on your completed journal pages every once in a while to identify patterns, monitor goals, and celebrate your progress.

Date: _____ / _____ / _____

○  ○ ○ ○ ○

SOCIAL MEDIA USAGE

	Goal Time:	**Actual Time:**

Instead of scrolling, liking, and posting, I...

○ Journaled
○ Spent time with friends
○ Meditated
○ Went outside
○ Learned something new
○ Cooked
○ Cleaned
○ Read
○ Played video games
○ Watched TV
○ _____
○ _____

Other:
_____

Today's Social Media Temperature:

MADE ME STRESSED/ ANGRY/SAD

MADE ME CALM/ HAPPY/MOTIVATED

END OF DAY REFLECTION

The most effective or enjoyable activity I did instead of using social media was ....

because ....
....
....

Today, using social media made me feel ....
....
....

My time not using social media made me feel ....
....
....

Tomorrow I will ....
....
....

Date: /   /

○ ○ ○ ○ ○ ☺

SOCIAL MEDIA USAGE

	Goal Time:	Actual Time:	Instead of scrolling, liking, and posting, I...

Goal Time: **Actual Time:**   **Instead of scrolling, liking, and posting, I...**

○ Journaled
○ Spent time with friends
○ Meditated
○ Went outside
○ Learned something new
○ Cooked
○ Cleaned
○ Read
○ Played video games
○ Watched TV
○ _____
○ _____

Other:

_____

Today's Social Media Temperature:

END OF DAY REFLECTION

MADE ME STRESSED/ANGRY/SAD

MADE ME CALM/HAPPY/MOTIVATED

The most effective or enjoyable activity I did instead of using social media was ....

because ....
....

Today, using social media made me feel ....
....

My time not using social media made me feel ....
....

Tomorrow I will ....
....

Date: / /

SOCIAL MEDIA USAGE

	Goal Time:	Actual Time:	Instead of scrolling, liking, and posting, I...

○ Journaled
○ Spent time with friends
○ Meditated
○ Went outside
○ Learned something new
○ Cooked
○ Cleaned
○ Read
○ Played video games
○ Watched TV

Other:

○ _____
○ _____

_____

Today's Social Media Temperature:

END OF DAY REFLECTION

The most effective or enjoyable activity I did instead of using social media was ....

because ....
....

Today, using social media made me feel ....
....

My time not using social media made me feel ....
....

Tomorrow I will ....
....

MADE ME STRESSED/ ANGRY/SAD

MADE ME CALM/ HAPPY/MOTIVATED

Date: /   /

○ ○ ○ ☺ ○ ☺ ○ ☺

	Goal Time:	Actual Time:	Instead of scrolling, liking, and posting, I...

○ Journaled

○ Spent time with friends

○ Meditated

○ Went outside

○ Learned something new

○ Cooked

○ Cleaned

○ Read

○ Played video games

○ Watched TV

Other:

_____

○ _____

○ _____

Today's Social Media Temperature:

MADE ME STRESSED/ ANGRY/SAD

MADE ME CALM/ HAPPY/MOTIVATED

The most effective or enjoyable activity I did instead of using social media was ....

....

because ....

....

....

Today, using social media made me feel ....

....

....

My time not using social media made me feel ....

....

....

Tomorrow I will ....

....

....

Date: / /

SOCIAL MEDIA USAGE

	Goal Time:	Actual Time:	Instead of scrolling, liking, and posting, I...
Instagram			O Journaled
TikTok			O Spent time with friends
Snapchat			O Meditated
Facebook			O Went outside
Twitter			O Learned something new

O Cooked
O Cleaned
O Read
O Played video games
O Watched TV

Other:
_____

O _____
O _____

Today's Social Media Temperature:

MADE ME STRESSED/ ANGRY/SAD

MADE ME CALM/ HAPPY/MOTIVATED

END OF DAY REFLECTION

The most effective or enjoyable activity I did instead of using social media was ....

because ....
....

Today, using social media made me feel ....
....

My time not using social media made me feel ....
....

Tomorrow I will ....
....

"Mindfulness is a way
of befriending ourselves
and our experience."

—JON KABAT-ZINN, PHD,
Author, professor, and founder of
mindfulness-based stress reduction
(MBSR)

Date: /   /

○ ○ ○   ○

	Goal Time:	Actual Time:	Instead of scrolling, liking, and posting, I...

- ○ Journaled
- ○ Spent time with friends
- ○ Meditated
- ○ Went outside
- ○ Learned something new
- ○ Cooked
- ○ Cleaned
- ○ Read
- ○ Played video games
- ○ Watched TV
- ○ _____
- ○ _____

Other:

_____

Today's Social Media Temperature:

MADE ME STRESSED/ ANGRY/SAD

MADE ME CALM/ HAPPY/MOTIVATED

The most effective or enjoyable activity I did instead of using social media was ....

....

because ....

....

....

Today, using social media made me feel ....

....

....

My time not using social media made me feel ....

....

....

Tomorrow I will ....

....

....

Date: /   /

SOCIAL MEDIA USAGE

Goal Time: **Actual Time:**   **Instead of scrolling, liking, and posting, I...**

○ Journaled
○ Spent time with friends
○ Meditated
○ Went outside
○ Learned something new
○ Cooked
○ Cleaned
○ Read
○ Played video games
○ Watched TV
○ _____
○ _____

Other:
_____

Today's Social Media Temperature:

MADE ME STRESSED/ ANGRY/SAD

MADE ME CALM/ HAPPY/MOTIVATED

END OF DAY REFLECTION

The most effective or enjoyable activity I did instead of using social media was ....

because ....
....
....

Today, using social media made me feel ....
....
....

My time not using social media made me feel ....
....
....

Tomorrow I will ....
....
....

Date: /   /

SOCIAL MEDIA USAGE

	Goal Time:	Actual Time:	Instead of scrolling, liking, and posting, I...

Instead of scrolling, liking, and posting, I...

- O Journaled
- O Spent time with friends
- O Meditated
- O Went outside
- O Learned something new
- O Cooked
- O Cleaned
- O Read
- O Played video games
- O Watched TV
- O _____
- O _____

Other:

_____

Today's Social Media Temperature:

END OF DAY REFLECTION

The most effective or enjoyable activity I did instead of using social media was ....

because ....

Today, using social media made me feel ....

My time not using social media made me feel ....

Tomorrow I will ....

MADE ME STRESSED/ ANGRY/SAD

MADE ME CALM/ HAPPY/MOTIVATED

Date: /   /

MORNING MOOD TRACKER

○ 😣 ○ 😟 ○ 😐 ○ 🙂 ○ 😊

SOCIAL MEDIA USAGE

	Goal Time:	Actual Time:	Instead of scrolling, liking, and posting, I...

Instead of scrolling, liking, and posting, I...

O Journaled
O Spent time with friends
O Meditated
O Went outside
O Learned something new
O Cooked
O Cleaned
O Read
O Played video games
O Watched TV
O _____
O _____

Other:
_____

Today's Social Media Temperature:

END OF DAY REFLECTION

The most effective or enjoyable activity I did instead of using social media was ....

because ....
....
....

Today, using social media made me feel ....
....
....

My time not using social media made me feel ....
....
....

Tomorrow I will ....
....
....

MADE ME STRESSED/ ANGRY/SAD

MADE ME CALM/ HAPPY/MOTIVATED

Date: / /

○ 😣 ○ 😕 ○ 😐 ○ 🙂 ○ 😊

SOCIAL MEDIA USAGE

Goal Time: **Actual Time:**   **Instead of scrolling, liking, and posting, I...**

○ Journaled
○ Spent time with friends
○ Meditated
○ Went outside
○ Learned something new
○ Cooked
○ Cleaned
○ Read
○ Played video games
○ Watched TV

Other: ○ _____

_____   ○ _____

Today's Social Media Temperature:

MADE ME STRESSED/ ANGRY/SAD

MADE ME CALM/ HAPPY/MOTIVATED

END OF DAY REFLECTION

The most effective or enjoyable activity I did instead of using social media was ....

because ....
....
....

Today, using social media made me feel ....
....

My time not using social media made me feel ....
....

Tomorrow I will ....
....

Date: /   /

○ ○ ○ ○ ○

SOCIAL MEDIA USAGE

Goal Time: **Actual Time:**   **Instead of scrolling, liking, and posting, I...**

○ Journaled
○ Spent time with friends
○ Meditated
○ Went outside
○ Learned something new
○ Cooked
○ Cleaned
○ Read
○ Played video games
○ Watched TV
○ _____
○ _____

Other:
_____

Today's Social Media Temperature:

MADE ME STRESSED/ ANGRY/SAD

MADE ME CALM/ HAPPY/MOTIVATED

END OF DAY REFLECTION

The most effective or enjoyable activity I did instead of using social media was ....

because ....
....
....

Today, using social media made me feel ....
....
....

My time not using social media made me feel ....
....
....

Tomorrow I will ....
....
....

> "Your present circumstances don't determine where you can go; they merely determine where you start."

—NIDO QUBEIN,
Businessman and motivational speaker

Date: /   /

○ ○ ○ ○ ○ 😃

SOCIAL MEDIA USAGE

	Goal Time:	Actual Time:	Instead of scrolling, liking, and posting, I...

Goal Time: **Actual Time:**   **Instead of scrolling, liking, and posting, I...**

○ Journaled
○ Spent time with friends
○ Meditated
○ Went outside
○ Learned something new
○ Cooked
○ Cleaned
○ Read
○ Played video games
○ Watched TV
○ _____
○ _____

Other:

_____

Today's Social Media Temperature:

MADE ME STRESSED/ ANGRY/SAD

MADE ME CALM/ HAPPY/MOTIVATED

END OF DAY REFLECTION

The most effective or enjoyable activity I did instead of using social media was ....

because ....
....
....

Today, using social media made me feel ....
....
....

My time not using social media made me feel ....
....
....

Tomorrow I will ....
....
....

Date: / /

○ 😫 ○ 🙁 ○ 😐 ○ 🙂 ○ 😊

SOCIAL MEDIA USAGE

Goal Time: **Actual Time:**   **Instead of scrolling, liking, and posting, I...**

O Journaled

O Spent time with friends

O Meditated

O Went outside

O Learned something new

O Cooked

O Cleaned

O Read

O Played video games

O Watched TV

Other:

O _____

_____

O _____

Today's Social Media Temperature:

END OF DAY REFLECTION

The most effective or enjoyable activity I did instead of using social media was ....

....

because ....

....

....

MADE ME STRESSED/ ANGRY/SAD

Today, using social media made me feel ....

....

....

MADE ME CALM/ HAPPY/MOTIVATED

My time not using social media made me feel ....

....

....

Tomorrow I will ....

....

....

Date: /   /

○ ○ ○ ○ ○

SOCIAL MEDIA USAGE

	Goal Time:	Actual Time:	Instead of scrolling, liking, and posting, I...

Instead of scrolling, liking, and posting, I...

○ Journaled
○ Spent time with friends
○ Meditated
○ Went outside
○ Learned something new
○ Cooked
○ Cleaned
○ Read
○ Played video games
○ Watched TV
○ _____
○ _____

Other:

_____

Today's Social Media Temperature:

MADE ME STRESSED/ ANGRY/SAD

MADE ME CALM/ HAPPY/MOTIVATED

END OF DAY REFLECTION

The most effective or enjoyable activity I did instead of using social media was ....

because ....
....
....

Today, using social media made me feel ....
....
....

My time not using social media made me feel ....
....
....

Tomorrow I will ....
....
....

Date: ___ / ___ / ___

○ ○ ○ ○ ○

SOCIAL MEDIA USAGE

	Goal Time:	Actual Time:

Goal Time: **Actual Time:**

Instead of scrolling, liking, and posting, I...

○ Journaled
○ Spent time with friends
○ Meditated
○ Went outside
○ Learned something new
○ Cooked
○ Cleaned
○ Read
○ Played video games
○ Watched TV
○ _____
○ _____

Other:
_____

Today's Social Media Temperature:

MADE ME STRESSED/ ANGRY/SAD

MADE ME CALM/ HAPPY/MOTIVATED

END OF DAY REFLECTION

The most effective or enjoyable activity I did instead of using social media was ....

because ....
....

Today, using social media made me feel ....
....

My time not using social media made me feel ....
....

Tomorrow I will ....
....

Date: /   /

○ ○ ○ ○ ○ 😊

SOCIAL MEDIA USAGE

	Goal Time:	**Actual Time:**	**Instead of scrolling, liking, and posting, I...**

Instead of scrolling, liking, and posting, I...

- ○ Journaled
- ○ Spent time with friends
- ○ Meditated
- ○ Went outside
- ○ Learned something new
- ○ Cooked
- ○ Cleaned
- ○ Read
- ○ Played video games
- ○ Watched TV
- ○ _____
- ○ _____

Other:

_____

Today's Social Media Temperature:

MADE ME STRESSED/ ANGRY/SAD

MADE ME CALM/ HAPPY/MOTIVATED

END OF DAY REFLECTION

The most effective or enjoyable activity I did instead of using social media was ....

because ....

....

Today, using social media made me feel ....

....

....

My time not using social media made me feel ....

....

....

Tomorrow I will ....

....

....

Date: /   /

MORNING MOOD TRACKER

○ ○ ○ ○ ○ 😊

SOCIAL MEDIA USAGE

| | Goal Time: | Actual Time: | Instead of scrolling, liking, and posting, I... |

Goal Time: **Actual Time:**   **Instead of scrolling, liking, and posting, I...**

- ○ Journaled
- ○ Spent time with friends
- ○ Meditated
- ○ Went outside
- ○ Learned something new
- ○ Cooked
- ○ Cleaned
- ○ Read
- ○ Played video games
- ○ Watched TV
- ○ _____
- ○ _____

Other:

_____

Today's Social Media Temperature:

MADE ME STRESSED/ ANGRY/SAD

MADE ME CALM/ HAPPY/MOTIVATED

END OF DAY REFLECTION

The most effective or enjoyable activity I did instead of using social media was ....

because ....
....

Today, using social media made me feel ....
....
....

My time not using social media made me feel ....
....
....

Tomorrow I will ....
....
....

"Live the actual moment.
Only this actual moment
is life."

—THÍCH NHẤT HẠNH,
Buddhist monk

Date: /   /

MORNING MOOD TRACKER

SOCIAL MEDIA USAGE

	Goal Time:	**Actual Time:**

Instead of scrolling, liking, and posting, I...

- ○ Journaled
- ○ Spent time with friends
- ○ Meditated
- ○ Went outside
- ○ Learned something new
- ○ Cooked
- ○ Cleaned
- ○ Read
- ○ Played video games
- ○ Watched TV
- ○ _____
- ○ _____

Other:

_____

Today's Social Media Temperature:

MADE ME STRESSED/ ANGRY/SAD

MADE ME CALM/ HAPPY/MOTIVATED

END OF DAY REFLECTION

The most effective or enjoyable activity I did instead of using social media was ....

because ....
....
....

Today, using social media made me feel ....
....
....

My time not using social media made me feel ....
....
....

Tomorrow I will ....
....
....

Date: /   /

MORNING MOOD TRACKER

 ○ ○ ○ ○

SOCIAL MEDIA USAGE

	Goal Time:	**Actual Time:**

Instead of scrolling, liking, and posting, I...

○ Journaled
○ Spent time with friends
○ Meditated
○ Went outside
○ Learned something new
○ Cooked
○ Cleaned
○ Read
○ Played video games
○ Watched TV

Other:

_____

○ _____
○ _____

Today's Social Media Temperature:

MADE ME STRESSED/ ANGRY/SAD

MADE ME CALM/ HAPPY/MOTIVATED

END OF DAY REFLECTION

The most effective or enjoyable activity I did instead of using social media was ....

because ....
....

Today, using social media made me feel ....
....

My time not using social media made me feel ....
....

Tomorrow I will ....
....

Date: /   /

MORNING MOOD TRACKER

○ 😫 ○ 😖 ○ 😐 ○ 🙂 ○ 😊

SOCIAL MEDIA USAGE

	Goal Time:	Actual Time:

Instead of scrolling, liking, and posting, I...

○ Journaled
○ Spent time with friends
○ Meditated
○ Went outside
○ Learned something new
○ Cooked
○ Cleaned
○ Read
○ Played video games
○ Watched TV
○ _____
○ _____

Other:
_____

Today's Social Media Temperature:

MADE ME STRESSED/ ANGRY/SAD

MADE ME CALM/ HAPPY/MOTIVATED

END OF DAY REFLECTION

The most effective or enjoyable activity I did instead of using social media was ....

because ....
....
....

Today, using social media made me feel ....
....
....

My time not using social media made me feel ....
....
....

Tomorrow I will ....
....
....

Date: / /

MORNING MOOD TRACKER

SOCIAL MEDIA USAGE

	Goal Time:	**Actual Time:**	**Instead of scrolling, liking, and posting, I...**
Instagram			O Journaled
TikTok			O Spent time with friends
Snapchat			O Meditated
Facebook			O Went outside
Twitter			O Learned something new
			O Cooked
			O Cleaned
			O Read
			O Played video games
			O Watched TV

Other:

_____

O _____

O _____

Today's Social Media Temperature:

MADE ME STRESSED/ ANGRY/SAD

MADE ME CALM/ HAPPY/MOTIVATED

END OF DAY REFLECTION

The most effective or enjoyable activity I did instead of using social media was ....

because ....
....
....

Today, using social media made me feel ....
....
....

My time not using social media made me feel ....
....
....

Tomorrow I will ....
....
....

Date: / /

○ ○ ○ ○  ○

Goal Time: **Actual Time:**   **Instead of scrolling, liking, and posting, I...**

○ Journaled
○ Spent time with friends
○ Meditated
○ Went outside
○ Learned something new
○ Cooked
○ Cleaned
○ Read
○ Played video games
○ Watched TV

Other:

○ _____
○ _____
_____

Today's Social Media Temperature:

MADE ME STRESSED/ ANGRY/SAD

MADE ME CALM/ HAPPY/MOTIVATED

The most effective or enjoyable activity I did instead of using social media was ....

because ....
....

Today, using social media made me feel ....
....

My time not using social media made me feel ....
....

Tomorrow I will ....
....
....

Date: /   /

SOCIAL MEDIA USAGE

	Goal Time:	Actual Time:	Instead of scrolling, liking, and posting, I...

Goal Time: **Actual Time:**   **Instead of scrolling, liking, and posting, I...**

○ Journaled
○ Spent time with friends
○ Meditated
○ Went outside
○ Learned something new
○ Cooked
○ Cleaned
○ Read
○ Played video games
○ Watched TV
○ _____
○ _____

Other:
_____

Today's Social Media Temperature:

MADE ME STRESSED/ ANGRY/SAD

MADE ME CALM/ HAPPY/MOTIVATED

END OF DAY REFLECTION

The most effective or enjoyable activity I did instead of using social media was ....

because ....
....

Today, using social media made me feel ....
....

My time not using social media made me feel ....
....

Tomorrow I will ....
....

"When we get too caught up in the busyness of the world, we lose connection with one another—and ourselves."

—JACK KORNFIELD,
Author and Buddhist teacher

Date: /   /

○ ○ ○ ○ ○ 🙂

SOCIAL MEDIA USAGE

Goal Time: **Actual Time:**   **Instead of scrolling, liking, and posting, I...**

○ Journaled
○ Spent time with friends
○ Meditated
○ Went outside
○ Learned something new
○ Cooked
○ Cleaned
○ Read
○ Played video games
○ Watched TV
○ _____
○ _____

Other:
_____

Today's Social Media Temperature:

MADE ME STRESSED/ANGRY/SAD

MADE ME CALM/HAPPY/MOTIVATED

END OF DAY REFLECTION

The most effective or enjoyable activity I did instead of using social media was ....

because ....
....
....

Today, using social media made me feel ....
....
....

My time not using social media made me feel ....
....
....

Tomorrow I will ....
....
....

Date: /   /

SOCIAL MEDIA USAGE

Goal Time: Actual Time: **Instead of scrolling, liking, and posting, I...**

O Journaled
O Spent time with friends
O Meditated
O Went outside
O Learned something new
O Cooked
O Cleaned
O Read
O Played video games
O Watched TV

Other:

O _____

O _____

_____

Today's Social Media Temperature:

END OF DAY REFLECTION

The most effective or enjoyable activity I did instead of using social media was ....

because ....
....

MADE ME STRESSED/ ANGRY/SAD

MADE ME CALM/ HAPPY/MOTIVATED

Today, using social media made me feel ....
....

My time not using social media made me feel ....
....

Tomorrow I will ....
....

Date: / /

MORNING MOOD TRACKER

○ 😣 ○ 😟 ○ 😐 ○ 😊 ○ 😄

SOCIAL MEDIA USAGE

	Goal Time:	Actual Time:	Instead of scrolling, liking, and posting, I...

○ Journaled
○ Spent time with friends
○ Meditated
○ Went outside
○ Learned something new
○ Cooked
○ Cleaned
○ Read
○ Played video games
○ Watched TV
○ _____
○ _____

Other:

_____

Today's Social Media Temperature:

END OF DAY REFLECTION

The most effective or enjoyable activity I did instead of using social media was ....

because ....

....

....

Today, using social media made me feel ....

....

My time not using social media made me feel ....

....

Tomorrow I will ....

....

....

MADE ME STRESSED/ ANGRY/SAD

MADE ME CALM/ HAPPY/MOTIVATED

Date: /   /

SOCIAL MEDIA USAGE

	Goal Time:	Actual Time:

Instead of scrolling, liking, and posting, I...

○ Journaled
○ Spent time with friends
○ Meditated
○ Went outside
○ Learned something new
○ Cooked
○ Cleaned
○ Read
○ Played video games
○ Watched TV
○ _____
○ _____

Other:
_____

Today's Social Media Temperature:

MADE ME STRESSED/ ANGRY/SAD

MADE ME CALM/ HAPPY/MOTIVATED

END OF DAY REFLECTION

The most effective or enjoyable activity I did instead of using social media was ....

because ....

....

Today, using social media made me feel ....

....

My time not using social media made me feel ....

....

....

Tomorrow I will ....

....

Date: /   /

MORNING MOOD TRACKER

○ 😣 ○ 😟 ○ 😐 ○ 🙂 ○ 😊

SOCIAL MEDIA USAGE

Goal Time: **Actual Time:**   **Instead of scrolling, liking, and posting, I...**

○ Journaled
○ Spent time with friends
○ Meditated
○ Went outside
○ Learned something new
○ Cooked
○ Cleaned
○ Read
○ Played video games
○ Watched TV
○ _____
○ _____

Other:

_____

Today's Social Media Temperature:

END OF DAY REFLECTION

The most effective or enjoyable activity I did instead of using social media was ....

because ....
....

Today, using social media made me feel ....
....

My time not using social media made me feel ....
....

Tomorrow I will ....
....

MADE ME STRESSED/ ANGRY/SAD

MADE ME CALM/ HAPPY/MOTIVATED

Date: / /

SOCIAL MEDIA USAGE

	Goal Time:	Actual Time:

Instead of scrolling, liking, and posting, I...

O Journaled
O Spent time with friends
O Meditated
O Went outside
O Learned something new
O Cooked
O Cleaned
O Read
O Played video games
O Watched TV
O _____
O _____

Other:
_____

Today's Social Media Temperature:

MADE ME STRESSED/ ANGRY/SAD

MADE ME CALM/ HAPPY/MOTIVATED

END OF DAY REFLECTION

The most effective or enjoyable activity I did instead of using social media was ....

because ....
....

Today, using social media made me feel ....
....

My time not using social media made me feel ....
....

Tomorrow I will ....
....

"Be where you are. Otherwise you will miss most of your life."

—GAUTAMA BUDDHA,
Religious leader and teacher

Date: /   /

SOCIAL MEDIA USAGE

	Goal Time:	Actual Time:	Instead of scrolling, liking, and posting, I...

Instead of scrolling, liking, and posting, I...

○ Journaled
○ Spent time with friends
○ Meditated
○ Went outside
○ Learned something new
○ Cooked
○ Cleaned
○ Read
○ Played video games
○ Watched TV
○ _____
○ _____

Other:

_____

Today's Social Media Temperature:

MADE ME STRESSED/ ANGRY/SAD

MADE ME CALM/ HAPPY/MOTIVATED

END OF DAY REFLECTION

The most effective or enjoyable activity I did instead of using social media was ....

because ....
....
....

Today, using social media made me feel ....
....
....

My time not using social media made me feel ....
....
....

Tomorrow I will ....
....
....

Date: /   /

SOCIAL MEDIA USAGE

	Goal Time:	**Actual Time:**	**Instead of scrolling, liking, and posting, I...**
			O Journaled
			O Spent time with friends
			O Meditated
			O Went outside
			O Learned something new
			O Cooked
			O Cleaned
			O Read
			O Played video games
			O Watched TV
Other:			O _____
_____			O _____

**Today's
Social Media
Temperature:**

MADE ME STRESSED/
ANGRY/SAD

MADE ME CALM/
HAPPY/MOTIVATED

END OF DAY REFLECTION

The most effective or enjoyable activity I did instead of using
social media was ....

because ....
....
....

Today, using social media made me feel ....
....
....

My time not using social media made me feel ....
....
....

Tomorrow I will ....
....
....

Date: /   /

	Goal Time:	Actual Time:	Instead of scrolling, liking, and posting, I...

Instead of scrolling, liking, and posting, I...

- ○ Journaled
- ○ Spent time with friends
- ○ Meditated
- ○ Went outside
- ○ Learned something new
- ○ Cooked
- ○ Cleaned
- ○ Read
- ○ Played video games
- ○ Watched TV

Other:

_____

- ○ _____
- ○ _____

Today's Social Media Temperature:

MADE ME STRESSED/ANGRY/SAD

MADE ME CALM/HAPPY/MOTIVATED

The most effective or enjoyable activity I did instead of using social media was ....

because ....
....
....

Today, using social media made me feel ....
....
....

My time not using social media made me feel ....
....
....

Tomorrow I will ....
....
....

Date: /   /

SOCIAL MEDIA USAGE

| | Goal Time: | Actual Time: | Instead of scrolling, liking, and posting, I... |

Goal Time: Actual Time: **Instead of scrolling, liking, and posting, I...**

O Journaled
O Spent time with friends
O Meditated
O Went outside
O Learned something new
O Cooked
O Cleaned
O Read
O Played video games
O Watched TV

Other:
O _____
_____
O _____

Today's Social Media Temperature:

The most effective or enjoyable activity I did instead of using social media was ....

because ....

....

Today, using social media made me feel ....

....

My time not using social media made me feel ....

....

Tomorrow I will ....

....

MADE ME STRESSED/ ANGRY/SAD

MADE ME CALM/ HAPPY/MOTIVATED

Date: /   /

Goal Time: **Actual Time:**   **Instead of scrolling, liking,**
and posting, I...

- O Journaled
- O Spent time with friends
- O Meditated
- O Went outside
- O Learned something new
- O Cooked
- O Cleaned
- O Read
- O Played video games
- O Watched TV
- O _____
- O _____

Other:

_____

Today's
Social Media
Temperature:

The most effective or enjoyable activity I did instead of using
social media was ....

because ....
....
....

Today, using social media made me feel ....
....
....

My time not using social media made me feel ....
....
....

Tomorrow I will ....
....
....

MADE ME STRESSED/
ANGRY/SAD

MADE ME CALM/
HAPPY/MOTIVATED

Date: /   /

SOCIAL MEDIA USAGE

| | **Goal Time:** | **Actual Time:** | **Instead of scrolling, liking, and posting, I...** |

○ Journaled
○ Spent time with friends
○ Meditated
○ Went outside
○ Learned something new
○ Cooked
○ Cleaned
○ Read
○ Played video games
○ Watched TV

Other:

○ _____
○ _____

_____

Today's Social Media Temperature:

END OF DAY REFLECTION

The most effective or enjoyable activity I did instead of using social media was ....

....

because ....

....

....

Today, using social media made me feel ....

....

....

My time not using social media made me feel ....

....

....

Tomorrow I will ....

....

....

MADE ME STRESSED/ ANGRY/SAD

MADE ME CALM/ HAPPY/MOTIVATED

"Deep human connection is...
the purpose and the result
of a meaningful life—and
it will inspire the most
amazing acts of love,
generosity, and humanity."

—MELINDA GATES,
Computer scientist and philanthropist

Date: /   /

MORNING MOOD TRACKER

SOCIAL MEDIA USAGE

	Goal Time:	Actual Time:	Instead of scrolling, liking, and posting, I...

○ Journaled

○ Spent time with friends

○ Meditated

○ Went outside

○ Learned something new

○ Cooked

○ Cleaned

○ Read

○ Played video games

○ Watched TV

Other:

○ _____

_____

○ _____

Today's Social Media Temperature:

END OF DAY REFLECTION

The most effective or enjoyable activity I did instead of using social media was ....

MADE ME STRESSED/ ANGRY/SAD

because ....
....
....

Today, using social media made me feel ....

MADE ME CALM/ HAPPY/MOTIVATED

....
....

My time not using social media made me feel ....
....
....

Tomorrow I will ....
....
....

Date: / /

○ ○ ○  ○ ○

SOCIAL MEDIA USAGE

Goal Time: **Actual Time:** **Instead of scrolling, liking, and posting, I...**

- ○ Journaled
- ○ Spent time with friends
- ○ Meditated
- ○ Went outside
- ○ Learned something new
- ○ Cooked
- ○ Cleaned
- ○ Read
- ○ Played video games
- ○ Watched TV
- ○ _____
- ○ _____

Other:

_____

Today's Social Media Temperature:

MADE ME STRESSED/ ANGRY/SAD

MADE ME CALM/ HAPPY/MOTIVATED

END OF DAY REFLECTION

The most effective or enjoyable activity I did instead of using social media was ....

because ....

Today, using social media made me feel ....

My time not using social media made me feel ....

Tomorrow I will ....

Date: /   /

MORNING MOOD TRACKER

○ ○ ☹ ○ 😐 ○ 🙂 ○ 😊

SOCIAL MEDIA USAGE

	Goal Time:	**Actual Time:**	**Instead of scrolling, liking, and posting, I...**

○ Journaled

○ Spent time with friends

○ Meditated

○ Went outside

○ Learned something new

○ Cooked

○ Cleaned

○ Read

○ Played video games

○ Watched TV

○ _____

○ _____

Other:

_____

Today's Social Media Temperature:

END OF DAY REFLECTION

The most effective or enjoyable activity I did instead of using social media was _____

because _____

Today, using social media made me feel _____

My time not using social media made me feel _____

Tomorrow I will _____

MADE ME STRESSED/ ANGRY/SAD

MADE ME CALM/ HAPPY/MOTIVATED

Date: /   /

Goal Time: **Actual Time:**   **Instead of scrolling, liking, and posting, I...**

○ Journaled
○ Spent time with friends
○ Meditated
○ Went outside
○ Learned something new
○ Cooked
○ Cleaned
○ Read
○ Played video games
○ Watched TV

Other: ○ _____
_____   ○ _____

Today's Social Media Temperature:

The most effective or enjoyable activity I did instead of using social media was _____

because _____

Today, using social media made me feel _____

My time not using social media made me feel _____

Tomorrow I will _____

MADE ME STRESSED/ ANGRY/SAD

MADE ME CALM/ HAPPY/MOTIVATED

Date: /   /

SOCIAL MEDIA USAGE

	Goal Time:	Actual Time:	Instead of scrolling, liking, and posting, I...

- O Journaled
- O Spent time with friends
- O Meditated
- O Went outside
- O Learned something new
- O Cooked
- O Cleaned
- O Read
- O Played video games
- O Watched TV
- O _____
- O _____

Other:

_____

Today's Social Media Temperature:

END OF DAY REFLECTION

The most effective or enjoyable activity I did instead of using social media was ....

because ....

....

....

Today, using social media made me feel ....

....

....

My time not using social media made me feel ....

....

....

Tomorrow I will ....

....

....

MADE ME STRESSED/ ANGRY/SAD

MADE ME CALM/ HAPPY/MOTIVATED

Date: /   /

○ ○ ○ ○ ○

SOCIAL MEDIA USAGE

Goal Time: **Actual Time:**   **Instead of scrolling, liking, and posting, I...**

○ Journaled
○ Spent time with friends
○ Meditated
○ Went outside
○ Learned something new
○ Cooked
○ Cleaned
○ Read
○ Played video games
○ Watched TV
○ _____
○ _____

Other:

_____

Today's Social Media Temperature:

MADE ME STRESSED/ ANGRY/SAD

MADE ME CALM/ HAPPY/MOTIVATED

END OF DAY REFLECTION

The most effective or enjoyable activity I did instead of using social media was _____

because _____
_____.

Today, using social media made me feel _____
_____.

My time not using social media made me feel _____
_____.

Tomorrow I will _____
_____.

"We need to remind ourselves of the beauty of human connection and of nature and pull ourselves out of devices for [a] moment and appreciate...what it is just to be human beings."

—OLIVIA WILDE,
Actress and filmmaker

Date: /   /

SOCIAL MEDIA USAGE

	Goal Time:	Actual Time:
⊙ (Instagram)		
♪ (TikTok)		
👻 (Snapchat)		
f (Facebook)		
🐦 (Twitter)		
Other:		
_____		

Instead of scrolling, liking, and posting, I...

- ○ Journaled
- ○ Spent time with friends
- ○ Meditated
- ○ Went outside
- ○ Learned something new
- ○ Cooked
- ○ Cleaned
- ○ Read
- ○ Played video games
- ○ Watched TV
- ○ _____
- ○ _____

Today's Social Media Temperature:

MADE ME STRESSED/ ANGRY/SAD

MADE ME CALM/ HAPPY/MOTIVATED

END OF DAY REFLECTION

The most effective or enjoyable activity I did instead of using social media was ....

because ....
....
....

Today, using social media made me feel ....
....

My time not using social media made me feel ....
....

Tomorrow I will ....
....
....

Date: /   /

SOCIAL MEDIA USAGE

	Goal Time:	Actual Time:	Instead of scrolling, liking, and posting, I...

Goal Time: **Actual Time:**   **Instead of scrolling, liking, and posting, I...**

- ○ Journaled
- ○ Spent time with friends
- ○ Meditated
- ○ Went outside
- ○ Learned something new
- ○ Cooked
- ○ Cleaned
- ○ Read
- ○ Played video games
- ○ Watched TV
- ○ _____
- ○ _____

Other:

_____

Today's Social Media Temperature:

MADE ME STRESSED/ ANGRY/SAD

MADE ME CALM/ HAPPY/MOTIVATED

END OF DAY REFLECTION

The most effective or enjoyable activity I did instead of using social media was ....

because ....

....

Today, using social media made me feel ....

....

My time not using social media made me feel ....

....

Tomorrow I will ....

....

Date: /   /

SOCIAL MEDIA USAGE

Goal Time: **Actual Time:**   **Instead of scrolling, liking, and posting, I...**

- ○ Journaled
- ○ Spent time with friends
- ○ Meditated
- ○ Went outside
- ○ Learned something new
- ○ Cooked
- ○ Cleaned
- ○ Read
- ○ Played video games
- ○ Watched TV
- ○ _____
- ○ _____

Other:

_____

Today's Social Media Temperature:

MADE ME STRESSED/ ANGRY/SAD

MADE ME CALM/ HAPPY/MOTIVATED

END OF DAY REFLECTION

The most effective or enjoyable activity I did instead of using social media was ....

because ....
....

Today, using social media made me feel ....
....

My time not using social media made me feel ....
....

Tomorrow I will ....
....

Date: /   /

SOCIAL MEDIA USAGE

| | Goal Time: | Actual Time: | Instead of scrolling, liking, and posting, I... |

Goal Time: **Actual Time:**

Instead of scrolling, liking, and posting, I...

- O Journaled
- O Spent time with friends
- O Meditated
- O Went outside
- O Learned something new
- O Cooked
- O Cleaned
- O Read
- O Played video games
- O Watched TV
- O _____
- O _____

Other:

_____

Today's Social Media Temperature:

MADE ME STRESSED/ ANGRY/SAD

MADE ME CALM/ HAPPY/MOTIVATED

END OF DAY REFLECTION

The most effective or enjoyable activity I did instead of using social media was ....

because ....
....
....

Today, using social media made me feel ....
....
....

My time not using social media made me feel ....
....
....

Tomorrow I will ....
....
....

Date: /   /

MORNING MOOD TRACKER

SOCIAL MEDIA USAGE

Goal Time: | **Actual Time:** | **Instead of scrolling, liking, and posting, I...**

(Instagram)

(TikTok)

(Snapchat)

(Facebook)

(Twitter)

Other:

_____

- O Journaled
- O Spent time with friends
- O Meditated
- O Went outside
- O Learned something new
- O Cooked
- O Cleaned
- O Read
- O Played video games
- O Watched TV
- O _____
- O _____

Today's Social Media Temperature:

MADE ME STRESSED/ ANGRY/SAD

MADE ME CALM/ HAPPY/MOTIVATED

END OF DAY REFLECTION

The most effective or enjoyable activity I did instead of using social media was ....

because ....
....

Today, using social media made me feel ....
....

My time not using social media made me feel ....
....

Tomorrow I will ....
....

Date: /   /

○  ○ 😠 ○ 😦 ○ 😐 ○ 🙂 ○ 😃

SOCIAL MEDIA USAGE

	Goal Time:	**Actual Time:**	**Instead of scrolling, liking, and posting, I...**

○ Journaled
○ Spent time with friends
○ Meditated
○ Went outside
○ Learned something new
○ Cooked
○ Cleaned
○ Read
○ Played video games
○ Watched TV
○ _____
○ _____

Other:

_____

Today's Social Media Temperature:

MADE ME STRESSED/ ANGRY/SAD

MADE ME CALM/ HAPPY/MOTIVATED

END OF DAY REFLECTION

The most effective or enjoyable activity I did instead of using social media was ....

because ....
....
....

Today, using social media made me feel ....
....
....

My time not using social media made me feel ....
....
....

Tomorrow I will ....
....
....

"[Social media] can be great in moments, but I would just be careful and allow yourself some time limits when you should use it and when not."

—SELENA GOMEZ,
Musician

Date: /   /

MORNING MOOD TRACKER

○ ○ ○ ○  ○

SOCIAL MEDIA USAGE

Goal Time: **Actual Time:**

Instead of scrolling, liking, and posting, I...

- ○ Journaled
- ○ Spent time with friends
- ○ Meditated
- ○ Went outside
- ○ Learned something new
- ○ Cooked
- ○ Cleaned
- ○ Read
- ○ Played video games
- ○ Watched TV
- ○ _____
- ○ _____

Other:

_____

Today's Social Media Temperature:

MADE ME STRESSED/ ANGRY/SAD

MADE ME CALM/ HAPPY/MOTIVATED

END OF DAY REFLECTION

The most effective or enjoyable activity I did instead of using social media was ....

....

because ....

....

....

Today, using social media made me feel ....

....

....

My time not using social media made me feel ....

....

....

Tomorrow I will ....

....

....

Date: /   /

MORNING MOOD TRACKER

○ 😣 ○ 🙁 ○ 😐 ○ 🙂 ○ 😊

SOCIAL MEDIA USAGE

	Goal Time:	Actual Time:	Instead of scrolling, liking, and posting, I...

(Instagram icon)
(TikTok icon)
(Snapchat icon)
(Facebook icon)
(Twitter icon)

Other:
_____

Instead of scrolling, liking, and posting, I...

○ Journaled
○ Spent time with friends
○ Meditated
○ Went outside
○ Learned something new
○ Cooked
○ Cleaned
○ Read
○ Played video games
○ Watched TV
○ _____
○ _____

Today's Social Media Temperature:

MADE ME STRESSED/ ANGRY/SAD

MADE ME CALM/ HAPPY/MOTIVATED

END OF DAY REFLECTION

The most effective or enjoyable activity I did instead of using social media was ....

because ....
....
....

Today, using social media made me feel ....
....
....

My time not using social media made me feel ....
....
....

Tomorrow I will ....
....
....

Date: /   /

SOCIAL MEDIA USAGE

Goal Time: **Actual Time:**   **Instead of scrolling, liking, and posting, I...**

O Journaled

O Spent time with friends

O Meditated

O Went outside

O Learned something new

O Cooked

O Cleaned

O Read

O Played video games

O Watched TV

O _____

O _____

Other:
_____

Today's Social Media Temperature:

MADE ME STRESSED/ ANGRY/SAD

MADE ME CALM/ HAPPY/MOTIVATED

END OF DAY REFLECTION

The most effective or enjoyable activity I did instead of using social media was ....

because ....

....

Today, using social media made me feel ....

My time not using social media made me feel ....

Tomorrow I will ....

....

Date: /   /

MORNING MOOD TRACKER

○ 😣 ○ 😦 ○ 😐 ○ 🙂 ○ 😃

SOCIAL MEDIA USAGE

Goal Time: **Actual Time:**

Instead of scrolling, liking, and posting, I...

○ Journaled
○ Spent time with friends
○ Meditated
○ Went outside
○ Learned something new
○ Cooked
○ Cleaned
○ Read
○ Played video games
○ Watched TV

Other:

_____

○ _____
○ _____

Today's Social Media Temperature:

MADE ME STRESSED/ ANGRY/SAD

MADE ME CALM/ HAPPY/MOTIVATED

END OF DAY REFLECTION

The most effective or enjoyable activity I did instead of using social media was ....

....

because ....

....

....

Today, using social media made me feel ....

....

....

My time not using social media made me feel ....

....

....

Tomorrow I will ....

....

....

Date: /   /

○ 😣 ○ 🙁 ○ 😐 ○ 🙂 ○ 😄

SOCIAL MEDIA USAGE

	Goal Time:	Actual Time:	Instead of scrolling, liking, and posting, I...

Goal Time: Actual Time: **Instead of scrolling, liking, and posting, I...**

○ Journaled
○ Spent time with friends
○ Meditated
○ Went outside
○ Learned something new
○ Cooked
○ Cleaned
○ Read
○ Played video games
○ Watched TV

Other:
_____

○ _____
○ _____

Today's Social Media Temperature:

END OF DAY REFLECTION

The most effective or enjoyable activity I did instead of using social media was _____

because _____
_____
_____.

Today, using social media made me feel _____
_____.

My time not using social media made me feel _____
_____.

Tomorrow I will _____
_____
_____.

MADE ME STRESSED/ ANGRY/SAD

MADE ME CALM/ HAPPY/MOTIVATED

Date: /   /

SOCIAL MEDIA USAGE

Goal Time: **Actual Time:**   **Instead of scrolling, liking, and posting, I...**

O Journaled

O Spent time with friends

O Meditated

O Went outside

O Learned something new

O Cooked

O Cleaned

O Read

O Played video games

O Watched TV

O _____

O _____

Other:

_____

Today's Social Media Temperature:

MADE ME STRESSED/ ANGRY/SAD

MADE ME CALM/ HAPPY/MOTIVATED

END OF DAY REFLECTION

The most effective or enjoyable activity I did instead of using social media was ....

because ....
....
....

Today, using social media made me feel ....
....
....

My time not using social media made me feel ....
....
....

Tomorrow I will ....
....
....

"It takes discipline not to let social media steal your time."

—ALEXIS OHANIAN,
Entrepreneur

Date: /   /

MORNING MOOD TRACKER

○ 😣 ○ 😟 ○ 😐 ○ 😊 ○ 😄

SOCIAL MEDIA USAGE

	Goal Time:	Actual Time:	Instead of scrolling, liking, and posting, I...

Instead of scrolling, liking, and posting, I...

- ○ Journaled
- ○ Spent time with friends
- ○ Meditated
- ○ Went outside
- ○ Learned something new
- ○ Cooked
- ○ Cleaned
- ○ Read
- ○ Played video games
- ○ Watched TV
- ○ _____
- ○ _____

Other:
_____

Today's Social Media Temperature:

MADE ME STRESSED/ ANGRY/SAD

MADE ME CALM/ HAPPY/MOTIVATED

END OF DAY REFLECTION

The most effective or enjoyable activity I did instead of using social media was ....

because ....
....
....

Today, using social media made me feel ....
....

My time not using social media made me feel ....
....

Tomorrow I will ....
....

Date: /   /

SOCIAL MEDIA USAGE

Goal Time: **Actual Time:**   **Instead of scrolling, liking, and posting, I...**

O Journaled
O Spent time with friends
O Meditated
O Went outside
O Learned something new
O Cooked
O Cleaned
O Read
O Played video games
O Watched TV
O _____
O _____

Other:

_____

Today's Social Media Temperature:

MADE ME STRESSED/ ANGRY/SAD

MADE ME CALM/ HAPPY/MOTIVATED

END OF DAY REFLECTION

The most effective or enjoyable activity I did instead of using social media was _____

because _____

_____

_____.

Today, using social media made me feel _____

_____.

My time not using social media made me feel _____

_____.

Tomorrow I will _____

_____

_____.

Date: / /

MORNING MOOD TRACKER

SOCIAL MEDIA USAGE

	Goal Time:	Actual Time:

Other:

_____

Instead of scrolling, liking, and posting, I...

O Journaled
O Spent time with friends
O Meditated
O Went outside
O Learned something new
O Cooked
O Cleaned
O Read
O Played video games
O Watched TV
O _____
O _____

Today's Social Media Temperature:

MADE ME STRESSED/ ANGRY/SAD

MADE ME CALM/ HAPPY/MOTIVATED

END OF DAY REFLECTION

The most effective or enjoyable activity I did instead of using social media was _____

because _____
_____ .

Today, using social media made me feel _____
_____ .

My time not using social media made me feel _____
_____ .

Tomorrow I will _____
_____ .

Date: /   /

Goal Time: **Actual Time:**   **Instead of scrolling, liking, and posting, I...**

- ○ Journaled
- ○ Spent time with friends
- ○ Meditated
- ○ Went outside
- ○ Learned something new
- ○ Cooked
- ○ Cleaned
- ○ Read
- ○ Played video games
- ○ Watched TV
- ○ _____
- ○ _____

Other:
_____

Today's Social Media Temperature:

MADE ME STRESSED/ ANGRY/SAD

MADE ME CALM/ HAPPY/MOTIVATED

The most effective or enjoyable activity I did instead of using social media was ....

because ....
....

Today, using social media made me feel ....
....

My time not using social media made me feel ....
....

Tomorrow I will ....
....

Date: /   /

○ 😞 ○ 🙁 ○ 😐 ○ 🙂 ○ 😊

SOCIAL MEDIA USAGE

	Goal Time:	Actual Time:	Instead of scrolling, liking, and posting, I...

Instead of scrolling, liking, and posting, I...

○ Journaled
○ Spent time with friends
○ Meditated
○ Went outside
○ Learned something new
○ Cooked
○ Cleaned
○ Read
○ Played video games
○ Watched TV
○ _____
○ _____

Other:
_____

Today's Social Media Temperature:

END OF DAY REFLECTION

The most effective or enjoyable activity I did instead of using social media was ....

....

because ....

....

....

Today, using social media made me feel ....

....

....

My time not using social media made me feel ....

....

....

Tomorrow I will ....

....

....

MADE ME STRESSED/ANGRY/SAD

MADE ME CALM/HAPPY/MOTIVATED

Date: /   /

     MORNING MOOD TRACKER

SOCIAL MEDIA USAGE

	Goal Time:	**Actual Time:**	**Instead of scrolling, liking, and posting, I...**

○ Journaled
○ Spent time with friends
○ Meditated
○ Went outside
○ Learned something new
○ Cooked
○ Cleaned
○ Read
○ Played video games
○ Watched TV

Other:

_____

○ _____
○ _____

Today's Social Media Temperature:

END OF DAY REFLECTION

The most effective or enjoyable activity I did instead of using social media was _____

because _____
_____ .

Today, using social media made me feel _____
_____ .

My time not using social media made me feel _____
_____ .

Tomorrow I will _____
_____ .

MADE ME STRESSED/ ANGRY/SAD

MADE ME CALM/ HAPPY/MOTIVATED

"Social media is one of the best places in the world and one of the worst—it counteracts itself. It sends such amazing messages; it raises awareness of situations that need to be heard....But then there are some really heartbreaking things to happen on social media and I have dealt with a lot of bullying online. I want to make it a happy place."

—MILLIE BOBBY BROWN,
Actress

Date: /   /

Goal Time: **Actual Time:**   **Instead of scrolling, liking, and posting, I...**

- O Journaled
- O Spent time with friends
- O Meditated
- O Went outside
- O Learned something new
- O Cooked
- O Cleaned
- O Read
- O Played video games
- O Watched TV

Other:

_____

- O _____
- O _____

Today's Social Media Temperature:

MADE ME STRESSED/ ANGRY/SAD

MADE ME CALM/ HAPPY/MOTIVATED

The most effective or enjoyable activity I did instead of using social media was ....

....

because ....

....

Today, using social media made me feel ....

....

My time not using social media made me feel ....

....

Tomorrow I will ....

....

Date: /   /

MORNING MOOD TRACKER

○ ○ ○ ○ ○

SOCIAL MEDIA USAGE

| | **Goal Time:** | **Actual Time:** | **Instead of scrolling, liking, and posting, I...** |

O Journaled

O Spent time with friends

O Meditated

O Went outside

O Learned something new

O Cooked

O Cleaned

O Read

O Played video games

O Watched TV

Other:

O _____

O _____

_____

Today's Social Media Temperature:

END OF DAY REFLECTION

The most effective or enjoyable activity I did instead of using social media was ....

because ....

....

....

Today, using social media made me feel ....

....

My time not using social media made me feel ....

....

Tomorrow I will ....

....

MADE ME STRESSED/ ANGRY/SAD

MADE ME CALM/ HAPPY/MOTIVATED

Date: /   /

○ ○ ○  ○ ○ 😊

SOCIAL MEDIA USAGE

	Goal Time:	Actual Time:	Instead of scrolling, liking, and posting, I...

Goal Time: **Actual Time:**   **Instead of scrolling, liking, and posting, I...**

- Journaled
- Spent time with friends
- Meditated
- Went outside
- Learned something new
- Cooked
- Cleaned
- Read
- Played video games
- Watched TV
- ○ _____
- ○ _____

Other:
_____

Today's Social Media Temperature:

MADE ME STRESSED/ANGRY/SAD

MADE ME CALM/HAPPY/MOTIVATED

END OF DAY REFLECTION

The most effective or enjoyable activity I did instead of using social media was ....

because ....
....
....

Today, using social media made me feel ....
....

My time not using social media made me feel ....
....

Tomorrow I will ....
....
....

Date: /   /

SOCIAL MEDIA USAGE

Goal Time: Actual Time: **Instead of scrolling, liking, and posting, I...**

○ Journaled
○ Spent time with friends
○ Meditated
○ Went outside
○ Learned something new
○ Cooked
○ Cleaned
○ Read
○ Played video games
○ Watched TV

Other:

○ _____
_____

○ _____

Today's Social Media Temperature:

END OF DAY REFLECTION

The most effective or enjoyable activity I did instead of using social media was ....

MADE ME STRESSED/ ANGRY/SAD

because ....
....
....

Today, using social media made me feel ....
....

MADE ME CALM/ HAPPY/MOTIVATED

My time not using social media made me feel ....
....
....

Tomorrow I will ....
....
....

Date: /   /

SOCIAL MEDIA USAGE

Goal Time: **Actual Time:**   **Instead of scrolling, liking, and posting, I...**

O Journaled
O Spent time with friends
O Meditated
O Went outside
O Learned something new
O Cooked
O Cleaned
O Read
O Played video games
O Watched TV
O _____
O _____

Other:
_____

Today's Social Media Temperature:

END OF DAY REFLECTION

The most effective or enjoyable activity I did instead of using social media was ....

because ....
....
....

Today, using social media made me feel ....
....
....

My time not using social media made me feel ....
....
....

Tomorrow I will ....
....
....

MADE ME STRESSED/ ANGRY/SAD

MADE ME CALM/ HAPPY/MOTIVATED

Date: /   /

○ 😫 ○ 🙁 ○ 😐 ○ 🙂 ○ 😃

SOCIAL MEDIA USAGE

Goal Time: **Actual Time:**

Instead of scrolling, liking, and posting, I...

○ Journaled
○ Spent time with friends
○ Meditated
○ Went outside
○ Learned something new
○ Cooked
○ Cleaned
○ Read
○ Played video games
○ Watched TV
○ _____
○ _____

Other:

_____

Today's Social Media Temperature:

MADE ME STRESSED/ ANGRY/SAD

MADE ME CALM/ HAPPY/MOTIVATED

END OF DAY REFLECTION

The most effective or enjoyable activity I did instead of using social media was _____

because _____

_____

Today, using social media made me feel _____

_____

My time not using social media made me feel _____

_____

Tomorrow I will _____

_____

"We don't have a choice on whether we do social media; the choice is how well we do it."

—ERIK QUALMAN,
Author

Date: /   /

MORNING MOOD TRACKER

SOCIAL MEDIA USAGE

	Goal Time:	Actual Time:	**Instead of scrolling, liking, and posting, I...**

Instead of scrolling, liking, and posting, I...

- ○ Journaled
- ○ Spent time with friends
- ○ Meditated
- ○ Went outside
- ○ Learned something new
- ○ Cooked
- ○ Cleaned
- ○ Read
- ○ Played video games
- ○ Watched TV
- ○ _____
- ○ _____

Other:

_____

Today's Social Media Temperature:

MADE ME STRESSED/ ANGRY/SAD

MADE ME CALM/ HAPPY/MOTIVATED

END OF DAY REFLECTION

The most effective or enjoyable activity I did instead of using social media was _____

because _____.

Today, using social media made me feel _____.

My time not using social media made me feel _____.

Tomorrow I will _____.

Date: /   /

SOCIAL MEDIA USAGE

Goal Time: **Actual Time:**   **Instead of scrolling, liking, and posting, I...**

- ○ Journaled
- ○ Spent time with friends
- ○ Meditated
- ○ Went outside
- ○ Learned something new
- ○ Cooked
- ○ Cleaned
- ○ Read
- ○ Played video games
- ○ Watched TV
- ○ _____
- ○ _____

Other:

_____

Today's Social Media Temperature:

MADE ME STRESSED/ ANGRY/SAD

MADE ME CALM/ HAPPY/MOTIVATED

END OF DAY REFLECTION

The most effective or enjoyable activity I did instead of using social media was

because

Today, using social media made me feel

My time not using social media made me feel

Tomorrow I will

Date: ___ / ___ / ___

○ ○ ○ ○ ○ ○

SOCIAL MEDIA USAGE

| | Goal Time: | Actual Time: | Instead of scrolling, liking, and posting, I... |

Goal Time: **Actual Time:**   **Instead of scrolling, liking, and posting, I...**

○ Journaled
○ Spent time with friends
○ Meditated
○ Went outside
○ Learned something new
○ Cooked
○ Cleaned
○ Read
○ Played video games
○ Watched TV

Other:

_____

○ _____

○ _____

Today's Social Media Temperature:

MADE ME STRESSED/ ANGRY/SAD

MADE ME CALM/ HAPPY/MOTIVATED

END OF DAY REFLECTION

The most effective or enjoyable activity I did instead of using social media was ....

because ....
....
....

Today, using social media made me feel ....
....
....

My time not using social media made me feel ....
....
....

Tomorrow I will ....
....
....

Date: /   /

Goal Time: **Actual Time:**   **Instead of scrolling, liking, and posting, I...**

O Journaled
O Spent time with friends
O Meditated
O Went outside
O Learned something new
O Cooked
O Cleaned
O Read
O Played video games
O Watched TV

Other: O _____

_____   O _____

Today's Social Media Temperature:

The most effective or enjoyable activity I did instead of using social media was ....

because ....
....
....

Today, using social media made me feel ....
....

My time not using social media made me feel ....
....

Tomorrow I will ....
....
....

MADE ME STRESSED/ ANGRY/SAD

MADE ME CALM/ HAPPY/MOTIVATED

Date: /   /

	Goal Time:	Actual Time:

Instead of scrolling, liking, and posting, I...

- O Journaled
- O Spent time with friends
- O Meditated
- O Went outside
- O Learned something new
- O Cooked
- O Cleaned
- O Read
- O Played video games
- O Watched TV

Other:

_____

O _____

O _____

Today's Social Media Temperature:

MADE ME STRESSED/ ANGRY/SAD

MADE ME CALM/ HAPPY/MOTIVATED

The most effective or enjoyable activity I did instead of using social media was _____

because _____
_____.

Today, using social media made me feel _____
_____.

My time not using social media made me feel _____
_____.

Tomorrow I will _____
_____.

Date: /   /

○ ○ ○ ○ ○

SOCIAL MEDIA USAGE

Goal Time: **Actual Time:**

Instead of scrolling, liking, and posting, I...

○ Journaled
○ Spent time with friends
○ Meditated
○ Went outside
○ Learned something new
○ Cooked
○ Cleaned
○ Read
○ Played video games
○ Watched TV
○ _____
○ _____

Other:

_____

Today's Social Media Temperature:

MADE ME STRESSED/ ANGRY/SAD

MADE ME CALM/ HAPPY/MOTIVATED

END OF DAY REFLECTION

The most effective or enjoyable activity I did instead of using social media was _____

because _____
_____ .

Today, using social media made me feel _____
_____
_____ .

My time not using social media made me feel _____
_____
_____ .

Tomorrow I will _____
_____
_____ .

"Even as you make progress, you need the discipline to keep from backtracking and sabotaging the success as it's happening."

—NIPSEY HUSSLE,
Musician

Date: / /

MORNING MOOD TRACKER

SOCIAL MEDIA USAGE

Goal Time:	Actual Time:	Instead of scrolling, liking, and posting, I...

○ Journaled
○ Spent time with friends
○ Meditated
○ Went outside
○ Learned something new
○ Cooked
○ Cleaned
○ Read
○ Played video games
○ Watched TV

Other:

○ _____
○ _____

_____

Today's
Social Media
Temperature:

END OF DAY REFLECTION

The most effective or enjoyable activity I did instead of using
social media was ....

MADE ME STRESSED/ ANGRY/SAD

because ....
....
....

MADE ME CALM/ HAPPY/MOTIVATED

Today, using social media made me feel ....
....
....

My time not using social media made me feel ....
....
....

Tomorrow I will ....
....
....

Date: / /

SOCIAL MEDIA USAGE

	Goal Time:	Actual Time:	Instead of scrolling, liking, and posting, I...

Instead of scrolling, liking, and posting, I...

- O Journaled
- O Spent time with friends
- O Meditated
- O Went outside
- O Learned something new
- O Cooked
- O Cleaned
- O Read
- O Played video games
- O Watched TV

Other:

_____

O _____

O _____

Today's Social Media Temperature:

MADE ME STRESSED/ ANGRY/SAD

MADE ME CALM/ HAPPY/MOTIVATED

END OF DAY REFLECTION

The most effective or enjoyable activity I did instead of using social media was ....

because ....

Today, using social media made me feel ....

My time not using social media made me feel ....

Tomorrow I will ....

Date: /   /

MORNING MOOD TRACKER

SOCIAL MEDIA USAGE

	Goal Time:	Actual Time:

Instead of scrolling, liking, and posting, I...

○ Journaled
○ Spent time with friends
○ Meditated
○ Went outside
○ Learned something new
○ Cooked
○ Cleaned
○ Read
○ Played video games
○ Watched TV
○ _____
○ _____

Other:

_____

Today's Social Media Temperature:

MADE ME STRESSED/ ANGRY/SAD

MADE ME CALM/ HAPPY/MOTIVATED

END OF DAY REFLECTION

The most effective or enjoyable activity I did instead of using social media was ....

because ....
....
....

Today, using social media made me feel ....
....
....

My time not using social media made me feel ....
....
....

Tomorrow I will ....
....
....

Date: /   /

○ ☹ ○ ☹ ○ ☺ ○ ☺ ○ ☺

SOCIAL MEDIA USAGE

Goal Time: **Actual Time:**   **Instead of scrolling, liking, and posting, I...**

○ Journaled
○ Spent time with friends
○ Meditated
○ Went outside
○ Learned something new
○ Cooked
○ Cleaned
○ Read
○ Played video games
○ Watched TV

Other:

_____

○ _____
○ _____

Today's Social Media Temperature:

MADE ME STRESSED/ ANGRY/SAD

MADE ME CALM/ HAPPY/MOTIVATED

END OF DAY REFLECTION

The most effective or enjoyable activity I did instead of using social media was ....

because ....
....

Today, using social media made me feel ....
....

My time not using social media made me feel ....
....

Tomorrow I will ....
....

Date: /   /

Goal Time: **Actual Time:**   **Instead of scrolling, liking, and posting, I...**

○ Journaled
○ Spent time with friends
○ Meditated
○ Went outside
○ Learned something new
○ Cooked
○ Cleaned
○ Read
○ Played video games
○ Watched TV

Other:

_____

○ _____
○ _____

Today's Social Media Temperature:

MADE ME STRESSED/ ANGRY/SAD

MADE ME CALM/ HAPPY/MOTIVATED

The most effective or enjoyable activity I did instead of using social media was ....

because ....

Today, using social media made me feel ....

My time not using social media made me feel ....

Tomorrow I will ....

PART THREE: RE-ENGAGING WITH SOCIAL MEDIA   125

Date: /   /

SOCIAL MEDIA USAGE

	Goal Time:	Actual Time:	Instead of scrolling, liking, and posting, I...

Instead of scrolling, liking, and posting, I...

- ○ Journaled
- ○ Spent time with friends
- ○ Meditated
- ○ Went outside
- ○ Learned something new
- ○ Cooked
- ○ Cleaned
- ○ Read
- ○ Played video games
- ○ Watched TV
- ○ _____
- ○ _____

Other:
_____

Today's Social Media Temperature:

MADE ME STRESSED/ ANGRY/SAD

MADE ME CALM/ HAPPY/MOTIVATED

END OF DAY REFLECTION

The most effective or enjoyable activity I did instead of using social media was ....

because ....
....

Today, using social media made me feel ....
....

My time not using social media made me feel ....
....

Tomorrow I will ....
....

"If you don't like something, change it. If you can't change it, change your attitude."

—MAYA ANGELOU,
Poet

Date: ___ / ___ / ___

SOCIAL MEDIA USAGE

Goal Time: **Actual Time:**   **Instead of scrolling, liking, and posting, I...**

O Journaled

O Spent time with friends

O Meditated

O Went outside

O Learned something new

O Cooked

O Cleaned

O Read

O Played video games

O Watched TV

O _____

O _____

Other:

_____

Today's Social Media Temperature:

MADE ME STRESSED/ ANGRY/SAD

MADE ME CALM/ HAPPY/MOTIVATED

END OF DAY REFLECTION

The most effective or enjoyable activity I did instead of using social media was _____

because _____

Today, using social media made me feel _____

My time not using social media made me feel _____

Tomorrow I will _____

Date: /   /

○ ○ ○ ○ ○

SOCIAL MEDIA USAGE

Goal Time: **Actual Time:**   **Instead of scrolling, liking, and posting, I...**

○ Journaled
○ Spent time with friends
○ Meditated
○ Went outside
○ Learned something new
○ Cooked
○ Cleaned
○ Read
○ Played video games
○ Watched TV

Other:

_____

○ _____
○ _____

Today's Social Media Temperature:

MADE ME STRESSED/ ANGRY/SAD

MADE ME CALM/ HAPPY/MOTIVATED

END OF DAY REFLECTION

The most effective or enjoyable activity I did instead of using social media was ....

because ....
....
....

Today, using social media made me feel ....
....

My time not using social media made me feel ....
....

Tomorrow I will ....
....
....

Date: /   /

○ ○ ○  ○ ○

SOCIAL MEDIA USAGE

	Goal Time:	Actual Time:	**Instead of scrolling, liking, and posting, I...**

Instead of scrolling, liking, and posting, I...

○ Journaled
○ Spent time with friends
○ Meditated
○ Went outside
○ Learned something new
○ Cooked
○ Cleaned
○ Read
○ Played video games
○ Watched TV
○ _____
○ _____

Other:

_____

Today's Social Media Temperature:

MADE ME STRESSED/ ANGRY/SAD

MADE ME CALM/ HAPPY/MOTIVATED

END OF DAY REFLECTION

The most effective or enjoyable activity I did instead of using social media was ....

because ....

Today, using social media made me feel ....

My time not using social media made me feel ....

Tomorrow I will ....

Date: ___ / ___ / ___

MORNING MOOD TRACKER

SOCIAL MEDIA USAGE

| | Goal Time: | Actual Time: | Instead of scrolling, liking, and posting, I... |

Goal Time: Actual Time: **Instead of scrolling, liking, and posting, I...**

○ Journaled
○ Spent time with friends
○ Meditated
○ Went outside
○ Learned something new
○ Cooked
○ Cleaned
○ Read
○ Played video games
○ Watched TV

Other:

_____

○ _____

○ _____

Today's Social Media Temperature:

MADE ME STRESSED/ ANGRY/SAD

MADE ME CALM/ HAPPY/MOTIVATED

END OF DAY REFLECTION

The most effective or enjoyable activity I did instead of using social media was _____

because _____

_____ .

Today, using social media made me feel _____

_____ .

My time not using social media made me feel _____

_____ .

Tomorrow I will _____

_____ .

Date: /   /

SOCIAL MEDIA USAGE

	Goal Time:	Actual Time:	Instead of scrolling, liking, and posting, I...
			O Journaled
			O Spent time with friends
			O Meditated
			O Went outside
			O Learned something new
			O Cooked
			O Cleaned
			O Read
			O Played video games
			O Watched TV

Other:

_____

O _____

O _____

Today's Social Media Temperature:

MADE ME STRESSED/ANGRY/SAD

MADE ME CALM/HAPPY/MOTIVATED

END OF DAY REFLECTION

The most effective or enjoyable activity I did instead of using social media was ....

because ....

....

Today, using social media made me feel ....

....

My time not using social media made me feel ....

....

Tomorrow I will ....

....

Date: /   /

SOCIAL MEDIA USAGE

	Goal Time:	Actual Time:	Instead of scrolling, liking, and posting, I...

O Journaled
O Spent time with friends
O Meditated
O Went outside
O Learned something new
O Cooked
O Cleaned
O Read
O Played video games
O Watched TV
O _____
O _____

Other:
_____

Today's Social Media Temperature:

MADE ME STRESSED/ ANGRY/SAD

MADE ME CALM/ HAPPY/MOTIVATED

END OF DAY REFLECTION

The most effective or enjoyable activity I did instead of using social media was ....

because ....
....
....

Today, using social media made me feel ....
....
....

My time not using social media made me feel ....
....
....

Tomorrow I will ....
....
....

> **"Time you enjoy wasting is not wasted time."**

—JOHN LENNON,
Musician

Date: /   /

SOCIAL MEDIA USAGE

	Goal Time:	Actual Time:	Instead of scrolling, liking, and posting, I...

○ Journaled
○ Spent time with friends
○ Meditated
○ Went outside
○ Learned something new
○ Cooked
○ Cleaned
○ Read
○ Played video games
○ Watched TV

Other:

_____

○ _____

○ _____

Today's Social Media Temperature:

MADE ME STRESSED/ ANGRY/SAD

MADE ME CALM/ HAPPY/MOTIVATED

END OF DAY REFLECTION

The most effective or enjoyable activity I did instead of using social media was ....

because ....
....

Today, using social media made me feel ....
....

My time not using social media made me feel ....
....

Tomorrow I will ....
....
....

Date: / /

SOCIAL MEDIA USAGE

	Goal Time:	Actual Time:	Instead of scrolling, liking, and posting, I...
			O Journaled
			O Spent time with friends
			O Meditated
			O Went outside
			O Learned something new
			O Cooked
			O Cleaned
			O Read
			O Played video games
			O Watched TV

Other:

_____

O _____

O _____

Today's Social Media Temperature:

MADE ME STRESSED/ ANGRY/SAD

MADE ME CALM/ HAPPY/MOTIVATED

END OF DAY REFLECTION

The most effective or enjoyable activity I did instead of using social media was _____

because _____

_____

_____ .

Today, using social media made me feel _____

_____

_____ .

My time not using social media made me feel _____

_____

_____ .

Tomorrow I will _____

_____

_____ .

Date: / /

○ ○ ○ ○ ○

SOCIAL MEDIA USAGE

Goal Time:	Actual Time:	Instead of scrolling, liking, and posting, I...

○ Journaled
○ Spent time with friends
○ Meditated
○ Went outside
○ Learned something new
○ Cooked
○ Cleaned
○ Read
○ Played video games
○ Watched TV
○ _____
○ _____

Other:
_____

Today's Social Media Temperature:

MADE ME STRESSED/ ANGRY/SAD

MADE ME CALM/ HAPPY/MOTIVATED

END OF DAY REFLECTION

The most effective or enjoyable activity I did instead of using social media was ....

because ....
....
....

Today, using social media made me feel ....
....
....

My time not using social media made me feel ....
....
....

Tomorrow I will ....
....
....

Date: / /

SOCIAL MEDIA USAGE

Goal Time: **Actual Time:**   **Instead of scrolling, liking, and posting, I...**

O Journaled

O Spent time with friends

O Meditated

O Went outside

O Learned something new

O Cooked

O Cleaned

O Read

O Played video games

O Watched TV

Other:

O _____

_____

O _____

Today's Social Media Temperature:

END OF DAY REFLECTION

The most effective or enjoyable activity I did instead of using social media was ....

because ....
....
....

Today, using social media made me feel ....
....
....

My time not using social media made me feel ....
....
....

Tomorrow I will ....
....
....

MADE ME STRESSED/ ANGRY/SAD

MADE ME CALM/ HAPPY/MOTIVATED

Date: /   /

○ ○ ○ ○ ○

SOCIAL MEDIA USAGE

Goal Time: **Actual Time:**   **Instead of scrolling, liking, and posting, I...**

○ Journaled
○ Spent time with friends
○ Meditated
○ Went outside
○ Learned something new
○ Cooked
○ Cleaned
○ Read
○ Played video games
○ Watched TV
○ _____
○ _____

Other:

_____

END OF DAY REFLECTION

Today's Social Media Temperature:

MADE ME STRESSED/ ANGRY/SAD

MADE ME CALM/ HAPPY/MOTIVATED

The most effective or enjoyable activity I did instead of using social media was _____

because _____

.

Today, using social media made me feel _____

.

My time not using social media made me feel _____

.

Tomorrow I will _____

.

Date: /   /

SOCIAL MEDIA USAGE

	Goal Time:	Actual Time:	Instead of scrolling, liking, and posting, I...

Instead of scrolling, liking, and posting, I...

O Journaled
O Spent time with friends
O Meditated
O Went outside
O Learned something new
O Cooked
O Cleaned
O Read
O Played video games
O Watched TV

Other:

O _____

O _____

_____

Today's Social Media Temperature:

MADE ME STRESSED/ ANGRY/SAD

MADE ME CALM/ HAPPY/MOTIVATED

END OF DAY REFLECTION

The most effective or enjoyable activity I did instead of using social media was ....

because ....
....
....

Today, using social media made me feel ....
....
....

My time not using social media made me feel ....
....
....

Tomorrow I will ....
....
....

"Be not afraid of discomfort. If you can't put yourself in a situation where you are uncomfortable then you will never grow. You will never change. You'll never learn."

—JASON REYNOLDS,
Author

Date: /   /

MORNING MOOD TRACKER

SOCIAL MEDIA USAGE

Goal Time: **Actual Time:**

Instead of scrolling, liking, and posting, I...

O Journaled
O Spent time with friends
O Meditated
O Went outside
O Learned something new
O Cooked
O Cleaned
O Read
O Played video games
O Watched TV
O _____
O _____

Other:

_____

Today's Social Media Temperature:

MADE ME STRESSED/ ANGRY/SAD

MADE ME CALM/ HAPPY/MOTIVATED

END OF DAY REFLECTION

The most effective or enjoyable activity I did instead of using social media was ....
....

because ....
....
....

Today, using social media made me feel ....
....

My time not using social media made me feel ....
....

Tomorrow I will ....
....
....

Date: /   /

SOCIAL MEDIA USAGE

Goal Time: **Actual Time:**   **Instead of scrolling, liking, and posting, I...**

○ Journaled
○ Spent time with friends
○ Meditated
○ Went outside
○ Learned something new
○ Cooked
○ Cleaned
○ Read
○ Played video games
○ Watched TV
○ _____
○ _____

Other:

_____

Today's Social Media Temperature:

MADE ME STRESSED/ANGRY/SAD

MADE ME CALM/HAPPY/MOTIVATED

END OF DAY REFLECTION

The most effective or enjoyable activity I did instead of using social media was ....

because ....

Today, using social media made me feel ....

My time not using social media made me feel ....

Tomorrow I will ....

Date: /   /

SOCIAL MEDIA USAGE

Goal Time: **Actual Time:**   **Instead of scrolling, liking, and posting, I...**

O Journaled

O Spent time with friends

O Meditated

O Went outside

O Learned something new

O Cooked

O Cleaned

O Read

O Played video games

O Watched TV

Other:

_____

O _____

O _____

Today's Social Media Temperature:

MADE ME STRESSED/ ANGRY/SAD

MADE ME CALM/ HAPPY/MOTIVATED

END OF DAY REFLECTION

The most effective or enjoyable activity I did instead of using social media was ....

because ....
....
....

Today, using social media made me feel ....
....
....

My time not using social media made me feel ....
....
....

Tomorrow I will ....
....
....

Date: /   /

SOCIAL MEDIA USAGE

Goal Time: **Actual Time:**   **Instead of scrolling, liking, and posting, I...**

O Journaled
O Spent time with friends
O Meditated
O Went outside
O Learned something new
O Cooked
O Cleaned
O Read
O Played video games
O Watched TV

Other:

O _____

O _____

____

Today's Social Media Temperature:

MADE ME STRESSED/ ANGRY/SAD

MADE ME CALM/ HAPPY/MOTIVATED

END OF DAY REFLECTION

The most effective or enjoyable activity I did instead of using social media was ....

because ....

Today, using social media made me feel ....

My time not using social media made me feel ....

Tomorrow I will ....

Date: ___ / ___ / ___

○ 😠 ○ 🙁 ○ 😐 ○ 🙂 ○ 😊

SOCIAL MEDIA USAGE

	Goal Time:	Actual Time:

Instead of scrolling, liking, and posting, I...

○ Journaled
○ Spent time with friends
○ Meditated
○ Went outside
○ Learned something new
○ Cooked
○ Cleaned
○ Read
○ Played video games
○ Watched TV

Other:
_____

○ _____
○ _____

Today's Social Media Temperature:

MADE ME STRESSED/ ANGRY/SAD

MADE ME CALM/ HAPPY/MOTIVATED

END OF DAY REFLECTION

The most effective or enjoyable activity I did instead of using social media was _____

because _____

Today, using social media made me feel _____

My time not using social media made me feel _____

Tomorrow I will _____

Date:　　/　　/

	Goal Time:	Actual Time:

Instead of scrolling, liking, and posting, I...

- O Journaled
- O Spent time with friends
- O Meditated
- O Went outside
- O Learned something new
- O Cooked
- O Cleaned
- O Read
- O Played video games
- O Watched TV

Other:
_____

O _____

O _____

Today's Social Media Temperature:

MADE ME STRESSED/ ANGRY/SAD

MADE ME CALM/ HAPPY/MOTIVATED

The most effective or enjoyable activity I did instead of using social media was ....

because ....
....
....

Today, using social media made me feel ....
....
....

My time not using social media made me feel ....
....
....

Tomorrow I will ....
....
....

"Well, when it comes to social media—there are just times I turn off the world, you know. There are just some times you have to give yourself space to be quiet, which means you've got to set those phones down."

—MICHELLE OBAMA,
Lawyer and former First Lady of the
United States

Date: /   /

○ ○ ☹ ○ 😐 ○ 🙂 ○ 😊

SOCIAL MEDIA USAGE

Goal Time: **Actual Time:**   **Instead of scrolling, liking, and posting, I...**

○ Journaled
○ Spent time with friends
○ Meditated
○ Went outside
○ Learned something new
○ Cooked
○ Cleaned
○ Read
○ Played video games
○ Watched TV

Other: ○ _____

_____   ○ _____

Today's Social Media Temperature:

END OF DAY REFLECTION

The most effective or enjoyable activity I did instead of using social media was _____

because _____
_____.

Today, using social media made me feel _____
_____.

My time not using social media made me feel _____
_____.

Tomorrow I will _____
_____.

MADE ME STRESSED/ ANGRY/SAD

MADE ME CALM/ HAPPY/MOTIVATED

Date: /   /

SOCIAL MEDIA USAGE

Goal Time: **Actual Time:**   **Instead of scrolling, liking, and posting, I...**

- O Journaled
- O Spent time with friends
- O Meditated
- O Went outside
- O Learned something new
- O Cooked
- O Cleaned
- O Read
- O Played video games
- O Watched TV
- O _____
- O _____

Other:

_____

Today's Social Media Temperature:

MADE ME STRESSED/ ANGRY/SAD

MADE ME CALM/ HAPPY/MOTIVATED

END OF DAY REFLECTION

The most effective or enjoyable activity I did instead of using social media was ....

because ....
....
....

Today, using social media made me feel ....
....
....

My time not using social media made me feel ....
....
....

Tomorrow I will ....
....
....

Date: /   /

	Goal Time:	Actual Time:

Instead of scrolling, liking, and posting, I...

- O Journaled
- O Spent time with friends
- O Meditated
- O Went outside
- O Learned something new
- O Cooked
- O Cleaned
- O Read
- O Played video games
- O Watched TV
- O _____
- O _____

Other:
_____

Today's Social Media Temperature:

MADE ME STRESSED/ANGRY/SAD

MADE ME CALM/HAPPY/MOTIVATED

The most effective or enjoyable activity I did instead of using social media was ....

because ....
....
....

Today, using social media made me feel ....
....
....

My time not using social media made me feel ....
....
....

Tomorrow I will ....
....
....

Date: /   /

SOCIAL MEDIA USAGE

Goal Time: **Actual Time:**   **Instead of scrolling, liking, and posting, I...**

- O Journaled
- O Spent time with friends
- O Meditated
- O Went outside
- O Learned something new
- O Cooked
- O Cleaned
- O Read
- O Played video games
- O Watched TV
- O _____
- O _____

Other:

_____

Today's Social Media Temperature:

END OF DAY REFLECTION

The most effective or enjoyable activity I did instead of using social media was

because

Today, using social media made me feel

My time not using social media made me feel

Tomorrow I will

MADE ME STRESSED/ ANGRY/SAD

MADE ME CALM/ HAPPY/MOTIVATED

Date: /   /

MORNING MOOD TRACKER

SOCIAL MEDIA USAGE

Goal Time: **Actual Time:**

Instead of scrolling, liking, and posting, I...

- O Journaled
- O Spent time with friends
- O Meditated
- O Went outside
- O Learned something new
- O Cooked
- O Cleaned
- O Read
- O Played video games
- O Watched TV
- O _____
- O _____

Other:

_____

Today's Social Media Temperature:

MADE ME STRESSED/ ANGRY/SAD

MADE ME CALM/ HAPPY/MOTIVATED

END OF DAY REFLECTION

The most effective or enjoyable activity I did instead of using social media was ....

because ....
....
....

Today, using social media made me feel ....
....

My time not using social media made me feel ....
....

Tomorrow I will ....
....
....

Date: /   /

SOCIAL MEDIA USAGE

Goal Time: **Actual Time:**   **Instead of scrolling, liking, and posting, I...**

O   Journaled
O   Spent time with friends
O   Meditated
O   Went outside
O   Learned something new
O   Cooked
O   Cleaned
O   Read
O   Played video games
O   Watched TV

Other:

O   _____
O   _____
_____

Today's Social Media Temperature:

END OF DAY REFLECTION

The most effective or enjoyable activity I did instead of using social media was ....

because ....

....

....

Today, using social media made me feel ....

....

My time not using social media made me feel ....

....

Tomorrow I will ....

....

....

MADE ME STRESSED/ ANGRY/SAD

MADE ME CALM/ HAPPY/MOTIVATED

"What is interesting is the power and the impact of social media....So we must try to use social media in a good way."

—MALALA YOUSAFZAI,
Activist and Nobel Peace Prize laureate

Date: /   /

○ ○ ○ ○ ○

SOCIAL MEDIA USAGE

Goal Time:　　**Actual Time:**　　**Instead of scrolling, liking, and posting, I...**

○ Journaled
○ Spent time with friends
○ Meditated
○ Went outside
○ Learned something new
○ Cooked
○ Cleaned
○ Read
○ Played video games
○ Watched TV

Other:

_____

○ _____

○ _____

Today's Social Media Temperature:

END OF DAY REFLECTION

The most effective or enjoyable activity I did instead of using social media was ....

because ....

....

Today, using social media made me feel ....

....

My time not using social media made me feel ....

....

Tomorrow I will ....

....

MADE ME STRESSED/ ANGRY/SAD

MADE ME CALM/ HAPPY/MOTIVATED

Date: / /

○ ○ ○  ○ ○

SOCIAL MEDIA USAGE

	Goal Time:	Actual Time:

Instead of scrolling, liking, and posting, I...

- ○ Journaled
- ○ Spent time with friends
- ○ Meditated
- ○ Went outside
- ○ Learned something new
- ○ Cooked
- ○ Cleaned
- ○ Read
- ○ Played video games
- ○ Watched TV

Other:

_____

○ _____

○ _____

Today's Social Media Temperature:

MADE ME STRESSED/ ANGRY/SAD

MADE ME CALM/ HAPPY/MOTIVATED

END OF DAY REFLECTION

The most effective or enjoyable activity I did instead of using social media was ....

....

because ....

....

....

....

Today, using social media made me feel ....

....

....

My time not using social media made me feel ....

....

....

Tomorrow I will ....

....

....

Date: / /

TODAY'S INTENTIONS

MORNING MOOD TRACKER

○ ○ ○ ○ ○ 😃

SOCIAL MEDIA USAGE

	Goal Time:	Actual Time:	Instead of scrolling, liking, and posting, I...

Instead of scrolling, liking, and posting, I...

○ Journaled
○ Spent time with friends
○ Meditated
○ Went outside
○ Learned something new
○ Cooked
○ Cleaned
○ Read
○ Played video games
○ Watched TV
○ _____
○ _____

Other:

_____

Today's Social Media Temperature:

MADE ME STRESSED/ ANGRY/SAD

MADE ME CALM/ HAPPY/MOTIVATED

END OF DAY REFLECTION

The most effective or enjoyable activity I did instead of using social media was ....

because ....
....
....

Today, using social media made me feel ....
....
....

My time not using social media made me feel ....
....
....

Tomorrow I will ....
....
....

Date: ___ / ___ / ___

MORNING MOOD TRACKER

SOCIAL MEDIA USAGE

	Goal Time:	Actual Time:

Instead of scrolling, liking, and posting, I...

O Journaled
O Spent time with friends
O Meditated
O Went outside
O Learned something new
O Cooked
O Cleaned
O Read
O Played video games
O Watched TV
O _____
O _____

Other:
_____

Today's Social Media Temperature:

MADE ME STRESSED/ ANGRY/SAD

MADE ME CALM/ HAPPY/MOTIVATED

END OF DAY REFLECTION

The most effective or enjoyable activity I did instead of using social media was ....

because ....
....
....

Today, using social media made me feel ....
....

My time not using social media made me feel ....
....
....

Tomorrow I will ....
....
....

Date: /   /

SOCIAL MEDIA USAGE

Goal Time: **Actual Time:**   **Instead of scrolling, liking, and posting, I...**

O Journaled

O Spent time with friends

O Meditated

O Went outside

O Learned something new

O Cooked

O Cleaned

O Read

O Played video games

O Watched TV

Other:

_____

O _____

O _____

Today's Social Media Temperature:

MADE ME STRESSED/ ANGRY/SAD

MADE ME CALM/ HAPPY/MOTIVATED

END OF DAY REFLECTION

The most effective or enjoyable activity I did instead of using social media was _____

because _____

Today, using social media made me feel _____

My time not using social media made me feel _____

Tomorrow I will _____

Date: /   /

SOCIAL MEDIA USAGE

	Goal Time:	Actual Time:

Instead of scrolling, liking, and posting, I...

- ○ Journaled
- ○ Spent time with friends
- ○ Meditated
- ○ Went outside
- ○ Learned something new
- ○ Cooked
- ○ Cleaned
- ○ Read
- ○ Played video games
- ○ Watched TV
- ○ _____
- ○ _____

Other:

_____

Today's Social Media Temperature:

MADE ME STRESSED/ ANGRY/SAD

MADE ME CALM/ HAPPY/MOTIVATED

END OF DAY REFLECTION

The most effective or enjoyable activity I did instead of using social media was ....

because ....
....
....

Today, using social media made me feel ....
....

My time not using social media made me feel ....
....
....

Tomorrow I will ....
....
....

"This social media era is giving us a more in-depth look at our favorite people, and it's all aspects, from music to movies to television to sports. I think it has been somewhat of a distraction at times, but also a huge benefit."

—MATT BARNES,
Professional basketball player

Date: /   /

SOCIAL MEDIA USAGE

	Goal Time:	Actual Time:

Instead of scrolling, liking, and posting, I...

- ○ Journaled
- ○ Spent time with friends
- ○ Meditated
- ○ Went outside
- ○ Learned something new
- ○ Cooked
- ○ Cleaned
- ○ Read
- ○ Played video games
- ○ Watched TV
- ○ _____
- ○ _____

Other:

_____

Today's Social Media Temperature:

MADE ME STRESSED/ ANGRY/SAD

MADE ME CALM/ HAPPY/MOTIVATED

END OF DAY REFLECTION

The most effective or enjoyable activity I did instead of using social media was ....

because ....
....
....

Today, using social media made me feel ....
....
....

My time not using social media made me feel ....
....
....

Tomorrow I will ....
....
....

Date: /   /

TODAY'S INTENTIONS

MORNING MOOD TRACKER

○ 😣 ○ 🙁 ○ 😐 ○ 🙂 ○ 😄

SOCIAL MEDIA USAGE

	Goal Time:	Actual Time:	Instead of scrolling, liking, and posting, I...

- ○ Journaled
- ○ Spent time with friends
- ○ Meditated
- ○ Went outside
- ○ Learned something new
- ○ Cooked
- ○ Cleaned
- ○ Read
- ○ Played video games
- ○ Watched TV
- ○ _____
- ○ _____

Other:
_____

Today's Social Media Temperature:

MADE ME STRESSED/ANGRY/SAD

MADE ME CALM/HAPPY/MOTIVATED

END OF DAY REFLECTION

The most effective or enjoyable activity I did instead of using social media was _____

because _____
_____ .

Today, using social media made me feel _____
_____ .

My time not using social media made me feel _____
_____ .

Tomorrow I will _____
_____ .

Date: / /

Goal Time: **Actual Time:**

Instead of scrolling, liking, and posting, I...

O Journaled
O Spent time with friends
O Meditated
O Went outside
O Learned something new
O Cooked
O Cleaned
O Read
O Played video games
O Watched TV
O _____
O _____

Other:

_____

Today's Social Media Temperature:

The most effective or enjoyable activity I did instead of using social media was ....

....

because ....

....
....

Today, using social media made me feel ....

....

My time not using social media made me feel ....

....
....

Tomorrow I will ....

....
....

MADE ME STRESSED/ ANGRY/SAD

MADE ME CALM/ HAPPY/MOTIVATED

Date: /   /

SOCIAL MEDIA USAGE

	Goal Time:	Actual Time:	Instead of scrolling, liking, and posting, I...

○ Journaled
○ Spent time with friends
○ Meditated
○ Went outside
○ Learned something new
○ Cooked
○ Cleaned
○ Read
○ Played video games
○ Watched TV
○ _____
○ _____

Other:

_____

Today's Social Media Temperature:

MADE ME STRESSED/ ANGRY/SAD

MADE ME CALM/ HAPPY/MOTIVATED

END OF DAY REFLECTION

The most effective or enjoyable activity I did instead of using social media was ....

because ....
....
....

Today, using social media made me feel ....
....

My time not using social media made me feel ....
....

Tomorrow I will ....
....
....

Date: /   /

	Goal Time:	**Actual Time:**

Instead of scrolling, liking, and posting, I...

- ○ Journaled
- ○ Spent time with friends
- ○ Meditated
- ○ Went outside
- ○ Learned something new
- ○ Cooked
- ○ Cleaned
- ○ Read
- ○ Played video games
- ○ Watched TV
- ○ _____
- ○ _____

Other:

_____

Today's Social Media Temperature:

MADE ME STRESSED/ ANGRY/SAD

MADE ME CALM/ HAPPY/MOTIVATED

The most effective or enjoyable activity I did instead of using social media was ....

because ....

....

Today, using social media made me feel ....

....

My time not using social media made me feel ....

....

Tomorrow I will ....

....

Date: /   /

○ 😦 ○ 🙁 ○ 😐 ○ 🙂 ○ 😄

SOCIAL MEDIA USAGE

	Goal Time:	Actual Time:

Instead of scrolling, liking, and posting, I...

- ○ Journaled
- ○ Spent time with friends
- ○ Meditated
- ○ Went outside
- ○ Learned something new
- ○ Cooked
- ○ Cleaned
- ○ Read
- ○ Played video games
- ○ Watched TV
- ○ _____
- ○ _____

Other:

_____

Today's Social Media Temperature:

MADE ME STRESSED/ ANGRY/SAD

MADE ME CALM/ HAPPY/MOTIVATED

END OF DAY REFLECTION

The most effective or enjoyable activity I did instead of using social media was ....

because ....

....

....

Today, using social media made me feel ....

....

....

My time not using social media made me feel ....

....

....

Tomorrow I will ....

....

....

"If you are on social media, and you are not learning, not laughing, not being inspired or not networking, then you are using it wrong."

—GERMANY KENT,
Journalist

Date: /   /

SOCIAL MEDIA USAGE

Goal Time: **Actual Time:**   **Instead of scrolling, liking, and posting, I...**

- O Journaled
- O Spent time with friends
- O Meditated
- O Went outside
- O Learned something new
- O Cooked
- O Cleaned
- O Read
- O Played video games
- O Watched TV
- O _____
- O _____

Other:
_____

Today's Social Media Temperature:

END OF DAY REFLECTION

The most effective or enjoyable activity I did instead of using social media was _____

because _____

Today, using social media made me feel _____

My time not using social media made me feel _____

Tomorrow I will _____

MADE ME STRESSED/ ANGRY/SAD

MADE ME CALM/ HAPPY/MOTIVATED

Date: /   /

Goal Time: **Actual Time:**   **Instead of scrolling, liking, and posting, I...**

O Journaled

O Spent time with friends

O Meditated

O Went outside

O Learned something new

O Cooked

O Cleaned

O Read

O Played video games

O Watched TV

Other:

O _____

_____

O _____

Today's Social Media Temperature:

The most effective or enjoyable activity I did instead of using social media was ....

because ....

....

....

Today, using social media made me feel ....

....

....

My time not using social media made me feel ....

....

....

Tomorrow I will ....

....

....

MADE ME STRESSED/ ANGRY/SAD

MADE ME CALM/ HAPPY/MOTIVATED

Date: /   /

Goal Time: **Actual Time:**   **Instead of scrolling, liking, and posting, I...**

O Journaled

O Spent time with friends

O Meditated

O Went outside

O Learned something new

O Cooked

O Cleaned

O Read

O Played video games

O Watched TV

Other:

_____

O _____

O _____

Today's Social Media Temperature:

MADE ME STRESSED/ ANGRY/SAD

MADE ME CALM/ HAPPY/MOTIVATED

The most effective or enjoyable activity I did instead of using social media was ....

because ....

....

Today, using social media made me feel ....

....

My time not using social media made me feel ....

....

Tomorrow I will ....

....

Date: /   /

MORNING MOOD TRACKER

SOCIAL MEDIA USAGE

	Goal Time:	Actual Time:	Instead of scrolling, liking, and posting, I...

○ Journaled

○ Spent time with friends

○ Meditated

○ Went outside

○ Learned something new

○ Cooked

○ Cleaned

○ Read

○ Played video games

○ Watched TV

○ _____

○ _____

Other:

_____

Today's Social Media Temperature:

MADE ME STRESSED/ ANGRY/SAD

MADE ME CALM/ HAPPY/MOTIVATED

END OF DAY REFLECTION

The most effective or enjoyable activity I did instead of using social media was ....

because ....

....

....

Today, using social media made me feel ....

....

My time not using social media made me feel ....

....

Tomorrow I will ....

....

....

Date: /   /

Goal Time: **Actual Time:**

Instead of scrolling, liking, and posting, I...

O Journaled
O Spent time with friends
O Meditated
O Went outside
O Learned something new
O Cooked
O Cleaned
O Read
O Played video games
O Watched TV
O _____
O _____

Other:
_____

Today's Social Media Temperature:

The most effective or enjoyable activity I did instead of using social media was ....

MADE ME STRESSED/ ANGRY/SAD

MADE ME CALM/ HAPPY/MOTIVATED

because ....

....

Today, using social media made me feel ....

....

My time not using social media made me feel ....

....

Tomorrow I will ....

....

Date: /   /

○ 😣 ○ 😖 ○ 😐 ○ 🙂 ○ 😊

SOCIAL MEDIA USAGE

	Goal Time:	Actual Time:	Instead of scrolling, liking, and posting, I...

○ Journaled
○ Spent time with friends
○ Meditated
○ Went outside
○ Learned something new
○ Cooked
○ Cleaned
○ Read
○ Played video games
○ Watched TV

Other:
_____

○ _____
○ _____

Today's Social Media Temperature:

END OF DAY REFLECTION

MADE ME STRESSED/ ANGRY/SAD

MADE ME CALM/ HAPPY/MOTIVATED

The most effective or enjoyable activity I did instead of using social media was ....

because ....
....
....

Today, using social media made me feel ....
....
....

My time not using social media made me feel ....
....
....

Tomorrow I will ....
....
....

"I'm fascinated by the idea that a human connection can be triggered through inanimate devices."

—VIRGIL ABLOH,
Fashion designer and entrepreneur